THE MAYFLOWER DESTINY

CYRIL LEEK MARSHALL

STACKPOLE BOOKS

THE MAYFLOWER DESTINY

Copyright ©1975 by
Cyril Leek Marshall

Published by
STACKPOLE BOOKS
Cameron and Kelker Streets
Harrisburg, Pa. 17105

Printed in the U.S.A.

Library of Congress Cataloging in Publication Data

Marshall, Cyril Leek, 1906-
    The Mayflower destiny.

    Bibliography: p.
    Includes index.
    1. Pilgrim Fathers.   2. Massachusetts—Social life and customs—Colonial period, ca. 1600-1775.   3. Massachusetts—History—Colonial period, ca. 1600-1775 (New Plymouth) I. Title.
F68.M37   974.4'02   75-19339
ISBN 0-8117-0998-1

*To Harry and
to Vera—
Both will know why.*

Contents

Preface

The Pilgrim story, now part of American folklore, is familiar to most Americans, and many in Britain. It is a story that has been told and retold by historians. Poets, playwrights, and script writers have used it, and experts in the fields of archaeology and architecture have given it new dimensions. Viewed through so many different eyes, the Pilgrims have loomed large, or small, depending on who is writing their story.

In 1957 a nonprofit organization, Plimoth Plantation, began to bring the Pilgrim story to life by building a replica Pilgrim village on a site closely resembling that of the original. Located about three miles from the center of Plymouth, on a hill above the Eel River, there is now a fort–meeting house and several cottages, arranged as they were in 1620 when the Pilgrims started their colony. Much research has gone into this project, some of which is contained in this book.

It was my privilege to be part of the team which made this village come to life, first by depicting scenes of Pilgrim life with costumed manikins placed in the houses already built. These I created by utilizing the knowledge we had of how the colonists looked and dressed. The houses were furnished with antiques, or reproductions of the many objects used in daily living. Eventually, the manikins in all but the fort were replaced by humans, who explained to visitors the many aspects of the Pilgrim story. At the present time, the visitor sees people in costume performing tasks in what is now a small farming community, with live animals and gardens being tended. This presents the Pilgrim story large as life, and the visitor may draw his own conclusions from confrontation with it.

In addition to the Pilgrim village, visitors to Plymouth may see a replica of the bark *Mayflower* moored at the State Pier, aboard which are shown costumed manikins in various aspects of Pilgrim life at sea. Insignificant as the Pilgrim story may seem to some, few see this ship without realizing what the Pilgrims must have suffered in their crossing to the land where they could be free to worship God in the manner of their choice.

It is for those who may never visit Plimoth Plantation that this book is written. The illustrations attempt to show that these colonists brought over with them their English way of life, building houses in the only way they knew how, that of medieval times. All their tools were European, their clothing was the fashion of their time, and their furnishings were solid and made to last. It was my task to find and get these furnishings made. Some reproductions were made in the Plimoth Plantation exhibits workshop; others were produced by craftsmen in England who worked in wood, clay, leather, and metal, in the manner of artisans of the seventeenth century. In time, several American craftsmen were found to make these reproductions.

In order to make sure that what was being reproduced was authentic in style, I made several trips to England, where I visited museums and talked to curators and keepers of print collections. These collections were most helpful in revealing aspects of life in the seventeenth century, and the many tools and artifacts used in daily living. I hope that all I discovered, much of which I show in the illustrations, will bring to my readers much of what they would see in a visit to Plimoth Plantation, since this was my reason for writing this book.

Acknowledgments

In writing this book I have borrowed largely from the standard works on the Pilgrims, from my own research, and from that of the research staff of Plimoth Plantation, including the archaeological department. I am indebted to all who helped me assemble the many exhibits in the Pilgrim village and aboard *Mayflower II*. I am particularly indebted to Henry Hornblower II, who, as he puts it, stole me away from St. Croix Museum in the Virgin Islands and gave me the opportunity, as exhibits director for Plimoth Plantation, to be a member of the team which created the Pilgrim village, the project he has guided as president for many years.

The author is indebted to Plimoth Plantation for the many photographs it supplied for this book. The reader should be cautioned, however, that such pictorial material does not imply that the directors of Plimoth Plantation endorse the contents of this book, about which they have no knowledge.

I was greatly helped in my research in England by Norman Cook, then keeper of the Guildhall Museum in London, and by John Waterer, then leather expert at the same institution. Both made known the likeliest places where I might find the information I sought. What I know about ships and navigation of the seventeenth century is due to David W. Waters, keeper of the Maritime Museum in Greenwich. Mr. Waters made the reproductions of seventeenth-century navigation instruments now aboard *Mayflower II*, as well as maps and globes used by mariners of that period. For other information on ships I must thank the American naval architect William A. Baker, who designed the replica *Mayflower*.

To the many keepers of folk museums and tool collections around England I owe much for my knowledge of tools used in the seventeenth century. For an intimate glimpse into the past I am indebted to the artists and printmakers of Holland and England who depicted the life and times of this period, and to keepers of paintings and prints who allowed me a closer look than the casual gallery visitor.

Finally, my thanks to those who encouraged me to write this book. I am grateful to my publisher for the opportunity to write and illustrate this book.

Chapter 1

European Explorations in the New World

CENTURIES before the Pilgrims crossed the Atlantic Ocean on the *Mayflower* in the year 1620, events which would lead to the discovery of America and other lands beyond were taking place in the world.

The first Europeans to reach the American continent were Norsemen. Setting out, in seemingly frail, open boats, they braved the cold northern reaches of the Arctic to discover first Iceland, then farther west, Greenland, where they established colonies. In A.D. 1000 exploring parties sailed even farther west, landing on the coast of a vast continent, later to be named North America. The various sites at which they landed are still being debated by historians, but evidence of settlements has been revealed by archaeologists. No great influx of Norsemen resulted from these landings, the settlers eventually returning to Greenland. Just why they could exist there, and not on the continent, is something we do not know. It may have been that they were driven out by others who had already set-

tled on the mainland, for we now know that a people of Asiatic origin did inhabit, over thousands of years, all of North and South America from the Arctic to Cape Horn. Our story does not concern these people until their contact with Europeans centuries later.

The years between 1000 and 1492 have been called the Dark Ages, a period when it seemed that human minds lay dormant. Of course, this was not true, since every age produces great people. Knowledge was restricted to a few in the societies that flourished, but not until the fifteenth century did enlightenment come to Europe, during the so-called Renaissance, or rebirth of learning. Then, in the universities scattered across that continent, scholars were at work retranslating the works of the ancient Greeks, unfolding long-forgotten ideas in such fields as astrology, geography, and philosophy. Added to this knowledge were the mathematical skills of the Arabs. In all of this accu-

SEVENTEENTH-CENTURY NAVIGATIONAL INSTRUMENTS

Shown here are part of the Alfred R. Meyer collection of reproductions of seventeenth-century navigational instruments, made by British craftsmen under the direction of David W. Waters, Deputy-Keeper, National Maritime Museum, Greenwich, England. All the instruments are usable.

mulated information lay the clues which enabled men to advance to greater things.

NAVIGATIONAL METHODS AND INSTRUMENTS

These clues included methods by which celestial bodies could be used to guide men across uncharted land and sea, aided by a magnetic compass which pointed roughly north, and an instrument to measure the angles of a star in relation to the earth's surface; the Arab mathematics were used to make such calculations, and proof that such methods worked was provided by the journeys made across Africa to the Orient. These trade routes to lands of riches and spices were open to those who could find their way, as Marco Polo, a Venetian traveler, did in the late thirteenth century, bringing back treasure from the realm of the great

Kublai Khan. Such trade routes were closed to the Christians of Europe when Moslem armies conquered the countries of the Middle East, despite efforts of the Crusaders to stop them. By the seventeenth century all land routes to the Orient were cut off, but long before this happened, other routes by sea were being sought. At first, efforts were concentrated on finding a way around the great continent of Africa. During this exploration much was learned about the best kinds of ships and sails for long voyages.

Although the best navigators of the fifteenth century may not have believed the old, prevailing myths concerning the terrors of travel out of the sight of land, in craft ill-suited to that purpose, many of the sailors under their command had such fears. Maps of the period were embellished with sea monsters and sirens who lured ships to destruction. Some sailors thought the world was flat, despite

Pythagoras's statement that it was a sphere. The known areas of the world could be found in a map in Ptolemy's *Geographica*. The size of the earth had been fairly accurately calculated by Eratosthenes, and Hipparchus declared that the earth revolved around the sun. Yet, despite this knowledge, it was not easy to find a willing crew to sign on for a long voyage.

PORTUGUESE EXPLORATIONS

With the invention of printing, first from blocks, then from movable type, the new knowledge became more available, and there were some who began to put it to practical use. One of these was

Prince Henry of Portugal (1394-1460), called The Navigator. Rich and scholarly, he instituted a seat of learning at Sagres, Portugal, to which he invited the leading scholars in the fields of astrology, geography, mathematics, and the sciences; in addition he employed cartographers and experienced navigators. Pooling their knowledge, and adding to it upon the completion of successful voyages made by Henry's ships, they drew up-to-date maps and charts on which they marked any new land discovered, and drew rhumb lines from which others could set a course when wishing to return to a given spot on the chart. The astrologers (forerunners of future astronomers) worked out tables based on star sights, and the navigators wrote manuals containing this information. Ships were modified or built

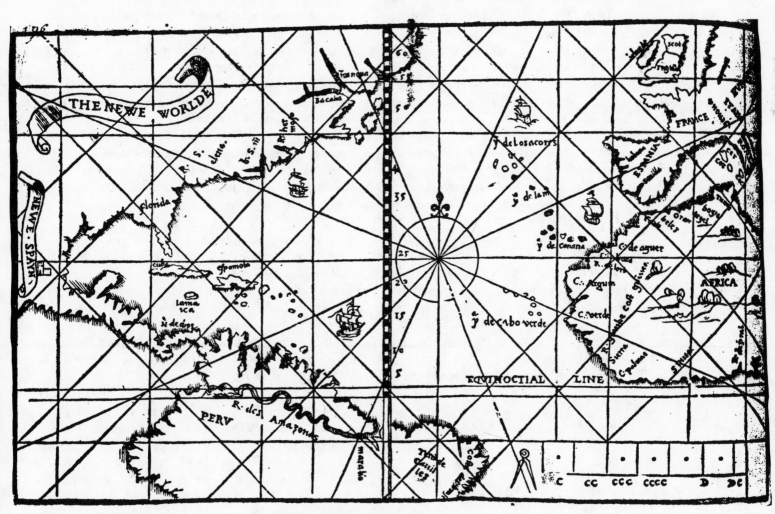

EARLY NAVIGATOR'S CHART

On this map of Europe and the New World rhumb lines, radiating from the compass, were drawn as an aid to the navigator in setting his course for a voyage.—*Photograph by Edward Leigh*

from scratch, incorporating hulls with new shapes to be used for long voyages. Sail plans were modified, and new rigs invented to take the best advantage of winds on trips to distant lands.

Full use was made of all these improvements, as Henry financed ventures, rewarding his captains for new discoveries. With the west coast of Africa as their target, Henry's captains pushed farther and farther toward the dread Tropic of Cancer, where sailors feared the sun would melt the tar out of their ships' seams, sinking them and drowning all in the boiling sea. It took Bartholomew Diáz to dispel this myth. In 1488, when he was driven by storms beyond the tip of Africa, he turned back north and found himself on the east coast of that great continent, having passed twice across the dreaded Tropic of Cancer without harm. His seamen balked at a continuance of the voyage and he was forced to make his way back home. Ten years later Vasco da Gama bettered the Diáz voyage by rounding the cape and sailing across to India. Prince Henry did not live to see this achievement. A new way had been found to the riches of the Orient, but again the Saracens barred the way.

The Portuguese seamen, many of them fishermen, were fine sailors who had ventured out of sight of land for generations. It is said that some had sailed across the Atlantic as far as the coast of South America, long before its discovery was officially announced. They had long visited the Cape Verde and Canary islands, which were far from their homeland in terms of distances sailed by ships of the fifteenth century. Other nations did not lag behind in terms of seamanship, as historical records show; Danish, English, and French ships had explored widely across the uncharted seas adjacent to their countries. The ancient Phoenicians had voyaged from their homeland as far as England to trade, but such voyages were not common in their time.

SEARCH FOR A NEW ROUTE TO THE ORIENT

Although Portugal fought to maintain a foothold on the East African and Indian coasts, it was costly in ships and men. A new way had to be found to the Orient, and the only way now indicated was by sailing westward across the Atlantic Ocean. This did not seem such a formidable undertaking if the map made by Toscanelli in 1474 could be believed. He showed the lands of Cipangu (Marco Polo's Japan) to be only a few weeks' sail across the Atlantic, and there was one man who believed him; this was Christopher Columbus, a Genoese seaman, who claimed a record of many voyages out of sight of land. He declared himself willing to make the voyage which would open up trade with the Orient.

It took some time for Columbus to get backing for his venture, but it was finally given by Spain, which put three ships at his disposal. Setting out on 3 August 1492, Columbus and his ships encountered mixed weather, but took advantage of favorable winds to get far out to sea. The voyage was not so short as Toscanelli's map had indicated. In fact, it took so long that the crews on the ships threatened mutiny if their leader did not turn back. Not to be thwarted, Columbus urged on his crew with promises of a reward for the first to sight land. Fortunately for Columbus, signs of land began to appear; sea birds and flotsam indicated a nearby land mass. This turned out to be the island called Guanahani by its inhabitants, but which Columbus called San Salvador.

Finding little of value there, Columbus sailed on, his crew now more encouraged about finding treasure somewhere ahead. The ships skirted a large island (Cuba), then sailed across to the north coast of a larger island, which Columbus named Hispaniola. Here his flagship *Santa Maria* was wrecked by drifting onto a reef. A post was established ashore and named La Navidad. With his supplies almost exhausted Columbus sailed back, via the Azores to Lisbon, where he was heaped with riches, titles, and honor. Backing for other trips was now easier to get, and Columbus made three more voyages, but ran into troubles too numerous to recount. He ended his days a broken man on 20 May 1506, but he died still believing that he had discovered the Indies. To this day the inhabitants of the lands he discovered are called Indians (i.e., West Indians). As a result of the discoveries made by Columbus, Spain laid claim to all lands across the Atlantic, later modifying her claims as Portugal sent explorers who discovered the great continent of South America.

Search for the Northwest Passage

When it was finally discovered that a large continent barred the way to the Orient, there were some who sought to find a passage around it, and many were to fail or die in attempts to locate one. With Spain and Portugal concentrating their efforts in the southern part of the Americas, it was up to someone to explore to the northwest to see what lay there. One such person was a spice merchant from Venice who located himself and family in the port of Bristol, England. Anglicizing his name to John Cabot, he set up in business. At the back of his mind was a plan to seek new sources for his stock-in-trade, spices. He was bold enough to petition King Henry VII for permission to make a voyage in search of a passage around America. This was granted, and with backing of Bristol merchants he procured a ship and crew, setting sail in 1497 to the northwest across the Atlantic. Cabot sighted, then went ashore on "Newe-founde-land," claiming it for England. Offshore he saw the sea teeming with fish. He had discovered the world's finest fishing grounds, the Grand Bank. Many countries later took advantage of this discovery, including the Catholic nations of Europe.

No record of Cabot's first voyage has been found, and how much other land he discovered remains a mystery. He did make it back home, and was able to get further backing, including five ships, on one of which he placed his son Sebastian. Some of Cabot's ships explored more extensively in the northwest, while Cabot went farther south, alert to find a promising opening which might be the passage he was seeking. John Cabot and his ship were lost at sea, but his son made it back home to become somewhat of a hero. He made many other voyages later, but in other parts of the world. There is no record of what became of the family spice business.

Space does not permit the recounting of the many voyages made across the Atlantic after Cabot. Spain sent explorers who penetrated the North American wilderness, some reaching the Pacific side overland. Spanish settlements were established in Florida, as a foothold in North America; but since the real wealth lay in the southern continent, Spain concentrated her efforts there, as did Portugal. Some remarkably long voyages were made along the coast of South America, Magellan finding his way through the straits named after him at the tip of the continent, and into the Pacific Ocean, which he sailed across, only to meet his death in the Philippine Islands. Some of his fleet made it back home after circumnavigating the world. Drake followed suit soon afterwards. Thus it can be seen that sailors were well able to undertake long voyages, and find their way back home, and accomplished this with really crude navigational instruments.

The French sent explorers to America, where they hoped to build settlements. They got a small foothold in Florida, but were driven out. Verrazano explored much of the North American coastline for France, followed by Cartier, who discovered the Gulf of Saint Lawrence, sailing up as far as the site of present-day Montreal. Here the French did settle with some success. No explorer had yet found a passage around the continent, but others were soon to try.

It would seem that the search for such a passage became an obsession with many of the explorers of the late sixteenth century. Icebergs and bitter weather did not seem to discourage them. They seemed almost to know that such a passage did exist, and they were right; but none ever got beyond the ice and many islands that were in that passage. Not until the year 1903 was this northwest passage successfully navigated, when Roald Amundsen, Norwegian Arctic explorer, did so in a small sloop, sailing on to Russia. A glance at a world globe will show why this passage eluded so many of the early explorers. Their names, at least, live on, having honored places on world maps. John Davis, who voyaged in 1585-87, found the entrance to the northwest passage, which is known as Davis Strait. Henry Hudson, who lost his life in the search, is remembered, Hudson Bay bearing his name. It was the persistence and dedication of these early explorers that made possible the ultimate colonization of America.

In the course of these voyages, much was discovered about the continent and its coastline. Maps, charts, and books were written, the latter stimulat-

SOME VOYAGES LEADING TO THE COLONIZATION OF NORTH AMERICA

Explorer	Birthplace	Year(s) of Exploration	Achievement
Leif Ericson	Iceland	1000	Sailing westward from Iceland, he discovered Labrador and Newfoundland and planted colonies at Vineland on the North American coast, but later abandoned them to return home.
Christopher Columbus	Italy	1492-1504	He discovered the Bahamas and other Caribbean islands. He never set foot on the mainland of North America.
John Cabot	Italy	1497-98	During two voyages under English patronage, he discovered Cape Breton Island, Nova Scotia, and Newfoundland.
Amerigo Vespucci	Italy	1497-98	He knew only the Florida coast in North America and concentrated his explorations along the coast of South America.
Gaspar Corte-Real	Portugal	1501	He explored Newfoundland and the northeast coast of North America.
Sebastian Cabot	Italy	1508-09	Seeking a northwest passage to the Indies, he voyaged to Labrador.
Ponce de Leon	Spain	1513	He discovered and named Florida.
Hernando Cortez	Spain	1519-36	He discovered Lower California.
Giovanni da Verrazano	Italy	1524	He discovered New York and Narragansett bays and explored the eastern coast of North America northward to Newfoundland.
Jacques Cartier	France	1534-35	He explored the west coast of Newfoundland and the Gulf of Saint Lawrence, sailing up as far as present-day Montreal.
Hernando de Soto	Spain	1539-42	He explored southeastern North America and the lower Mississippi Valley.
Francisco de Coronado	Spain	1540-42	He traced the Colorado River northward, discovered the Grand Canyon, and explored southern California, New Mexico, northern Texas, Oklahoma, and eastern Kansas.
Sir Martin Frobisher	England	1576-78	He discovered Frobisher Bay and Hudson Strait.
Samuel de Champlain	France	1603-13	He explored the Saint Lawrence River and the eastern coast of North America southward from Nova Scotia to Vineyard Haven. He founded and named Quebec, and discovered Lake Champlain.
Henry Hudson	England	1609-10	He discovered the Hudson River and the bay named for him.
Jacques Marquette and Louis Joliet	France	1673	They discovered Lake Michigan and explored the Wisconsin and Mississippi rivers.
Robert de la Salle	France	1682	He traced the Mississippi River to the Gulf of Mexico.

ing rich men to back seafaring ventures which might result in the finding of precious metals. Frobisher made a series of voyages to North America, taking back tons of what he thought was gold, only to discover it was iron pyrites, so-called fool's gold. It was to fool many others who came after him.

SIR WALTER RALEIGH AND THE ROANOKE COLONY

The accumulated knowledge about America led to the more sensible idea of colonization. Reports of abundant forests and arable land made the idea seem feasible. In consequence, a series of voyages were made to pick the choicest sites on which to establish colonies. In Queen Elizabeth's reign Sir Humphrey Gilbert made such a voyage, and as a result he got backing and ships, with 260 men aboard. Some of the ships sailed to Newfoundland, while Sir Humphrey voyaged farther south. He never returned, but his half-brother, Sir Walter Raleigh, who was on one of the ships, was inspired to continue Gilbert's search, and was granted a patent by his queen to found a colony in the New World.

A favorite of the queen, Raleigh was forbidden to make the voyage himself; so he appointed two of his friends, Richard Grenville and Ralph Lane, as leaders in his place. They sailed on 27 April 1584, taking advantage of winds that took them to the Caribbean, where they scouted for signs of Spanish defenses. They then headed up the coast of North America, sailing into a sound on the coast of present-day North Carolina. There they found an island, now called Roanoke Island, which seemed to be an ideal site for a settlement. The Indians they met were friendly, which was encouraging. Having decided that this site was ideal, Grenville and Lane sailed their ship back to England to make their report.

Raleigh was delighted with their choice, and named it Virginia, in honor of his virgin queen. He also started to organize a colonizing expedition, and placed the same two men in charge. Grenville was captain and Lane the colony leader. They sailed on 9 April 1585 for their chosen island site, making the voyage safely. With the colonists ashore Grenville took his ship back to England for further supplies. Just what went wrong is not known, but soon there was trouble with the Indians. The colony members were discouraged enough so that when Drake stopped off at their site, after a raiding expedition in the West Indies, they accepted his offer to take them back with him to England. Grenville in the meanwhile was bringing supplies but, on landing at Roanoke, he found the colony deserted. Not wishing to abandon it, he left fifteen of his men there, and sailed back home.

Another expedition, led by John White, an artist-recorder, arrived at Roanoke on 22 July 1587, but found no trace of Grenville's men. After putting ashore the new colonists, White returned to England for more supplies, only a week after the birth of his grandchild, Virginia Dare, the first child to be born in America of English parentage. It was unfortunate for this new colony that, at the time of White's return, England was menaced by an armada from Spain, and so pressed into service any available ship to build up her defenses. It was not until 17 August 1590 that White could return to the colony at Roanoke. He found the place in ruins, with no trace of any of the colonists. After a vain search on other islands he was forced to return home. What happened to the ill-fated colonists remains a mystery. Thus ended the first attempts at colonization. Not until the year 1606 was another attempt made, and this too was abortive.

THE LONDON AND PLYMOUTH COMPANIES

George Waymouth, sailing under the auspices of the Earl of Southampton and the latter's Roman Catholic son-in-law, Thomas Arundel, ostensibly to found a colony for Catholics, who found their position at home insecure, headed for Nantucket and the Maine coast. As a result of this voyage, two companies were issued patents; one was the London Company, the other the Plymouth Company, each backed by merchants of their respective cities. These were both so-called Virginia companies, the one from London being granted lands in a region between thirty-four degrees and forty-one degrees north, with the Plymouth Company rights between thirty-eight degrees and forty-five degrees north; but neither was to settle within 100 miles of the other. Each was to receive lands 50 miles north and south of its settlement, and 100 miles into the interior.

THE SETTLEMENT OF JAMESTOWN

As a result of these patents the London Company dispatched three ships which reached Virginia on 26 April 1607, entering Chesapeake Bay and discharging the colonists ashore at a place they named Jamestown. As had previously happened, troubles soon began. Their site was unhealthy, many dying from fevers. Lack of adequate food supplies caused others to die of starvation, leaving only thirty-two alive. Two supply ships arrived, one in January, the other in April of 1608, with other colonists aboard. Captain John Smith, one of their leaders, made strict rules, including one that denied food to those who did not work. Smith saw to the planting of crops, as a means of self-sustenance. As the colony progressed, military rule was changed to a form of self-government, but a succession of poor governors did not help the morale of the colonists, nor did their prospects seem bright until a newly arrived member brought with him tobacco seeds. In time tobacco became the cash crop, and the colony began to prosper. The introduction of this crop by John Rolfe was to make fortunes for planters and backers alike. Rolfe married the Indian maid Pocahontas, daughter of chief Powhatan, who had interceded with her father to save the life of the offending John Smith. Smith left Jamestown to explore for other colony sites. We shall meet with him again as our story progresses. When he left, the future of the colony was assured. Eventually, other successful colonies were planted along the North American coast. We will now see how these came about, and who made them possible.

EXPLORATION AND COLONIZATION ATTEMPTS IN NEW ENGLAND

New names began to appear on maps of the New World as explorers discovered new islands, bays, and rivers. On a voyage made in 1602, Bar-

Chronology of European Settlements in North America

Florida	1565	Spanish
Acadia	1605	French
Virginia	1607	English
Quebec	1608	French
Massachusetts	1620	English
New Amsterdam	1621	Dutch
New Hampshire	1623	English
Barbados	1625	English
Maryland	1633	English
Connecticut	1635	English
Rhode Island	1636	English
Banks of the Delaware	1637	Swedish
The Carolinas	1655	English
New Jersey	1664	English
New York	1664	English
Louisiana	1680	French
Delaware	1682	English
Pennsylvania	1682	English
Pennsylvania	1683	German
Texas (later part of Spanish province of Mexico)	1692	Spanish
Mississippi Valley	1699	French
Georgia	1732	English
California	1769	Spanish

tholomew Gosnold named Cape Cod, for obvious reasons, and Martha's Vineyard, after his daughter, and for the sea-grapes that abounded there.

A serious attempt at colonization was made in 1606 by the Plymouth Company, sponsored by Sir John Popham and Sir Ferdinando Gorges, with two ships, *Gift of God* and *Mary and John,* the former commanded by George Popham, the latter by Raleigh Gilbert. They sailed separately across the Atlantic a month apart, meeting on the Maine coast at the mouth of the Kennebec River, then known as the Sagadahoc. Ashore they picked a site and started building a fort, storehouse, and houses. Strange as it may seem, these colonists acted much like those at Jamestown, working little and quarreling among themselves. A hard winter did not help matters. By spring many had died, including their leader, George Popham. This so discouraged the remaining colonists that they decided to abandon their settlement and sail home. This they did, some sailing home the small pinnace they had built for use in trading. No further attempts were made to colonize for some time to come.

THE VOYAGES OF HENRY HUDSON

Many well-intentioned voyagers visited America in the seventeenth century, but others were out for personal gain, or were financed by merchants seeking quick profits. Henry Hudson, an English navigator, was hired by the Dutch to find a northwest passage through North America. Humane though he was, there were occasions when his treatment of Indians was questionable. Thwarted by ice and a near-mutinous crew, Hudson sailed southward, possibly as far as Virginia, and on his way back north he entered a large bay. There he lost an old shipmate to Indian arrows. This event may have incensed his seamen, since they were harsh with other Indians who tried to steal from them. Hudson sailed up the river which was named after him, penetrating as far as the present site of Albany. Realizing this was not a northwest passage, he turned back downstream and returned to England. He was not allowed to report to his Dutch employers, England wishing to profit from his voyage. Hudson was to die during a later search for a northwest passage. His name was given to the large bay he discovered in icy Arctic waters.

FRENCH ATTEMPTS AT COLONIZATION

The French were the next to attempt a colony, sending out a ship on which was a Jesuit priest, Father Briard, intent on converting the Indians to the Roman Catholic faith. Landing at the deserted colony on the Sagadahoc River, they thought to settle there, but chose a better site farther up the coast. Later other settlers gained a small foothold on this same coast, but all the settlements were destroyed by Captain Samuel Argall, sent up from Jamestown to eliminate French settlements in North America. On his way back to Jamestown, Argall called in at Manhattan Island, where the Dutch had established a trading post under Adriaen Block. This he took for England, but it was the Dutch who later colonized the Hudson River valley to profit from fur trading with the Indians.

THE COLONIZING IDEAS OF JOHN SMITH

One more explorer needs to be mentioned. As a leader at Jamestown, Captain John Smith had proved his worth, and we meet him again in the seas off the New England coast, where he was engaged in fishing and fur trading. Smith desperately wished to found a colony somewhere along this coast, his idea being to place yards there in which ships could be built and serviced for use in fishing and trading. He saw possibilities for the manufacture of naval stores from the tars of the pine trees that grew there in profusion. Smith's ideas were sound, but he never was able to get backing for them; perhaps his flamboyant personality, which was made evident in books he wrote about his many adventures, was against him. Smith even tried to persuade the Pilgrims to hire him as their leader when they were about to venture across the Atlantic to found a colony. Had they chosen him, they might have fared better than they did during the first few years of their life in America although Myles Standish, the leader they did choose, turned out to be of great help to them. It is now time to find out more about these founders of the first permanent colony in New England, and examine their reasons for leaving their homes, first in England, then Holland, to face unknown terrors in a strange land.

Chapter 2

The Pilgrim Identity

THE founders of the Jamestown colony seem particularly inept if compared with the organizers of a present-day expedition, for which the choice of the right personnel and adequate logistics are considered vital to success. To Jamestown went gentlemen-adventurers and an ill-assorted group of individuals, few of whom were skilled in the cultivation of land or fitted for the tasks of building. Some were riff-raff from the streets, only too glad to escape possible jail sentences. Supplies for the colonists were never sufficient to last until the next supply ship came, and few knew how to live off the land. In consequence, the colony almost failed several times, before good leaders turned the tide toward success. The Jamestown settlers sought for the most part, easy fortune, to be obtained by finding gold or other treasure. To turn a profit was essential to success, but first a way had to be found, either by planting cash crops or trading in commodities afforded by the country in which the settlement was made. It was a different kind of motivation that made possible the colony established at Plymouth by the Pilgrims in 1620, one we shall cover in some depth in the pages that follow.

In order to get backing for their colonizing venture, the Pilgrims had to enter into an agreement with their backers, who had profit primarily in mind. Monetary gain, however, was not the real motivation of the Pilgrims. Theirs was the stronger drive of religion, and a desire to practice it in their own way. To understand this driving force we must backtrack in history to find the events that transpired in the religious life of England which made the Pilgrims' course imperative.

THE PURITANS AND THE SEPARATISTS

It all started with Martin Luther, who sought to reform the Church of Rome. His preachings and writings seeped into England, and Henry VIII took advantage of them for his own purpose; but, in doing so, he unleashed a movement that swept through the British Isles, eventually resulting in the formation of splinter groups with their own ideas on how God should be worshipped, and the Bible be interpreted. Within the established church there were those who sought to purify it and strip it of any feature that reflected Rome and the Popé. These were the so-called Puritans. There were others who felt that only a completely new approach could be accepted and, seeing no hope for this, left the church to hold meetings of their own. These were the Separatists. The latter were by no means a homogeneous group under one leader, but were separated from each other by interpretative differences.

THE PILGRIMS' EXODUS TO HOLLAND

One stronghold of separatism was located at the juncture of the three counties of York, Nottingham, and Lincoln, in the little towns of Gainsborough, Scrooby, and Austerfield. Members of this group were leaders of the Pilgrims in England, Holland, and eventually the New World. At the manor house in Scrooby lived William Brewster, acting postmaster for the town. A retired diplomatic secretary, Brewster was an educated man who attracted to his house other scholars, graduates of Cambridge University; among them were John Smyth, Richard Clyfton, and John Robinson, the latter two being ordained ministers of the Anglican Church. Attracted to this group was the youthful William Bradford, who would emerge as the leader of the Plymouth colony. This little group attracted others sympathetic to their views, swelling the number meeting at Scrooby. In time their meetings were raided by church and civil authorities, and some went to jail for defying the established church. Eventually, life became intolerable to those who sought to worship God in their own way, and they cast their eyes toward Holland, a country more tolerant in outlook than the England of that day.

The first effort at escape ended in failure, and jail for some. On another attempt, made at night, the escaping party was separated by mischance, the men sailing away and leaving their families behind. Before too long they all managed to escape and

were reunited in Amsterdam. Very soon it became evident that the Scrooby group's ideas did not coincide with those of the group already settled there; so they moved to Leyden on 12 February 1609, having been granted permission to do so by the city authorities. Leyden was a wise choice, since the university there attracted the best of scholars and students, with whom the Pilgrims had contact, their own leaders attracting others of like mind.

THE LEYDEN CONGREGATION

The Leyden congregation appointed Robinson their spiritual leader, with Brewster serving as elder. These two men were a strength to their flock, inasmuch as life was not easy for them in Leyden. Forbidden entrance to the trade guilds, most were forced to work at more lowly trades and menial tasks to earn a living. Their housing was poor until a large house was provided for them to use as a meeting place and home for their pastor, around which were erected smaller houses for the flock. The town authorities, impressed by the exemplary conduct of the Pilgrims, contrasted it with that of other refugees, whose behavior left much to be desired.

The original congregation of about one hundred swelled to more than double as time went on. John Carver and Samuel Fuller joined them, and were to loom large when the move was made from Holland to the New World. Carver would be their first governor, and Fuller their physician; the latter was to prove himself as a healer when sickness struck the colony shortly after its establishment.

THE PILGRIMS' SEARCH FOR A COLONY SITE

When the younger members of the congregation became young men, there were fears for their well-being. Temptations were all around them, and they were influenced by the Dutch life, to the point that it was feared they would not stay English. Another place had to be found in which to live and worship in their own way. The leaders looked to the colonies which might be available to them in America. They rejected the Guiana site that Sir Walter Raleigh had praised, thinking it foreign to their nature as English people, too hot, and possibly fever-ridden. They also rejected an offer to go to New Netherland on the Hudson River, since they wished to remain English. Only then did the Pilgrims look to the English colonies as the one such place left to them. In Virginia there was land available to them, but not at Jamestown. There they would be subject to church rule. Seeking the advice of their pastor and elders, they found them receptive to a move to the New World; the Pilgrim leaders, in turn, appointed John Carver and Robert Cushman as agents to cross over to England in order to seek backing from the London Company, which had financed the Jamestown colony. Permission was also to be sought from the authorities for the group to worship in their own way, in whatever place they would settle; this would not be an easy problem to resolve. Nor did their agents find it easy to get backing; their negotiations were both long and difficult. Fortunately, the Pilgrim leaders were of steadfast character and not easy to be discouraged.

THE PILGRIM LEADERS

From a letter written by Robinson and Brewster we gain an insight into the nature of the Pilgrim fathers and others at Leyden. They wrote: "We are well weaned from the delicate milk of our mother country, and inured to the difficulties of a strange and hard land [Holland], which yet in great part we have by patience overcome. Lastly, it is not with us as with other men, whom small things can discourage, or small discontents cause to wish themselves at home again." All were equally determined to assume this same attitude when facing a new and harder life in America. That they thought of themselves as Pilgrims is revealed in the words of Bradford, as they prepared to depart from Holland: "So they left that good and pleasant city [Leyden] which had been their resting place twelve years; but they knew they were pilgrims." There is no doubt that their faith in God was very strong, and they believed He was on their side and would sustain them, no matter what their need. This faith, along with courage and sheer endurance allowed the strongest of them to survive sickness and near-starvation, and go on to success and, in some cases, wealth. Since the quality of the Pilgrims' leadership

played such an important part in the eventual success of their Plymouth colony, let us try to assess the strengths of the Pilgrim leaders.

William Brewster

William Brewster, who was fifty-three years old when he left for America, was a man of strong religious faith, as evidenced in the following words, which he wrote some time after the voyage: "In our heaviest trials has not Divine Presence ever been with us? . . . Generations to come shall look back to this hour, and these scenes of agonizing trial . . . and say: here was our beginning as a people. These were our fathers. Through their trials we inherit our blessings."

Brewster was also an educated man, a Cambridge University graduate, with experience in diplomatic affairs, some of which took him to Holland. He took over his father's duties as bailiff and postmaster at Scrooby Manor, and the Separatists held their meetings at his house. Threats of trouble with church and civil authorities caused the group to move to Holland. Brewster was married, and had six children before 1620. At Leyden he was appointed an elder of the congregation. He is reputed to have been a ribbon-maker in Leyden, but he also ran a clandestine printing business, publishing religious tracts, some of which landed him in serious trouble with the English authorities, who sought his arrest. In due course he agreed that the flock should seek freedom in the New World, and with sorrow and reluctance he and his wife, and sons Love and Wrestling, together with two indentured boys, sailed on the *Mayflower* to America. In the new colony Brewster was a source of strength to all. In the words of Bradford, "God gave good success to his indeavors herein all his days, and he saw the fruit of his labours in that behalf." Brewster died in 1644 at the age of seventy-seven, in spite of the fact that Bradford accounted him "not so fit for many employments as others were, especially such as were toilsome and laborious."

William Bradford

A man very close to Brewster was William Bradford, who as a youth had sought to find a way to worship his God in his own way, and realized it in the meetings of the Separatists at Scrooby Manor; he was seventeen at the time. When the move to Holland was made, he went along. Of scholarly bent, he mastered five foreign languages, including Hebrew and Greek. At Leyden he had contact with scholars at the university, and was himself a diligent reader. All this stood him in good stead when he wrote his history of Plymouth Plantation. Although written in hindsight rather than as a day-to-day journal, it reveals much about Pilgrim life in the Plymouth colony. However, Bradford left out much that could tell us the many things we would like to know about life in the Pilgrim village. These omissions leave a gap in their history that may now never be filled. While in Amsterdam, Bradford married; his wife Dorothy was later to drown when the *Mayflower* anchored off the tip of Cape Cod (Provincetown), an event which greatly saddened Bradford.

Bradford was a born leader and, after the death of the first governor of the colony, John Carver, in April 1621, he was elected to fill the vacancy. He served as governor every year, except five, until his death in Plymouth in 1657. Under Bradford's rule the colony was made self-governing. Although there were troubles along the way, he was able to deal with his people and with the Indians so that all lived in peace for many years, some prospering as a result of their hard work and abilities. Bradford's history is a classic work. The original version was lost for many years, finally turning up in the library of the bishop of London. It now reposes in a glass case at the State Library in the State House, Boston, Massachusetts.

John Carver

Little is known about John Carver, first governor of the Pilgrims. Yorkshire-born, he became a merchant of some consequence, and was thought to have put money into the colonial venture. He was forty-four when he embarked aboard the *Mayflower*. A member of the Leyden congregation, he helped negotiate the Pilgrims' deal with the London Adventurers. He took his wife, Katherine, and six servants with him to America, where most of them died, save John Howland, whose narrow

escape from drowning on the voyage over, we shall recount. In the colony, despite his position as governor, Carver pulled his weight. It was while at work planting in April 1621 that he complained of a severe headache, then fell senseless in the field and died. It might be said that, forsaking a life of comfort in England, he gave up all to practice freedom of religion in the wilds of America.

Myles Standish

We have seen that the Pilgrims had, in Brewster, Bradford, and Carver, men of stout purpose and strong religious motivation; all were members of the Leyden group and had already had their share of suffering in Holland, but the Pilgrims needed a military leader as well as spiritual mentors. Previous colonial ventures had included such a person; in Jamestown this had been Captain John Smith. Smith had offered his services to the Pilgrims, and he might have been a good choice, having served well in Virginia. Moreover, he knew the New England coast well, and had made a good map of that area, a copy of which the Pilgrims took with them. However, Smith was turned down, the Pilgrims choosing instead a Lancashire soldier who had served in Holland. He was not a Separatist, and never did join the Pilgrim congregation; but he was an upright man, and served them well as military leader, surveyor, contact man with the Indians, and helper in time of need. His detractors called him "little shrimp" on account of his small size. He had a temper, and was no man to antagonize. He proved himself brave on many occasions, especially in dealings with the Indians. He must have been a good trader, since when he died at his Duxbury farm in 1656, he left an estate worth £360 to his wife and four sons. Standish befriended the Indian Hobomok, who lived on his estate until his death. In addition to their God, the Pilgrims had a bulwark of strength in Myles Standish, and he served them well.

Isaac Allerton

The Pilgrims had, from time to time, to deal with their backers in England, and their only way to do this was to send over one of their number as agent. One such was Isaac Allerton, in his early thirties, a

man with keen bargaining instincts which later
made him the first merchant of New England. The
Leyden burghers thought enough of him to make
him a citizen, as they did Bradford, and his
brother-in-law, Degory Priest. Allerton married
Mary Norris in 1611, but she died at Plymouth the
first year. He did not marry again until 1627, at
which time he took as his bride Fear, daughter of
William Brewster. In all, Allerton made five
voyages to England to represent the colonists. At
Plymouth he served as an assistant to the governor,
a post which was equivalent to deputy governor.
He was one of several who became "undertakers,"
assuming the still outstanding debt to the Adventurers. In later years Allerton established a fish
business in Marblehead, but turned it over to his
son-in-law to run, while he attended to other business matters. These included dealings with the
Dutch at New Amsterdam, where he resided for a
time. He settled finally at New Haven, to which he
took the wife he married after the death of Fear.
Towards the end of his life Allerton suffered business reverses, and when he died his estate was
worth little. Thus, in 1658 Allerton passed away,
after serving the Pilgrims well.

John Alden

One Pilgrim known to most is John Alden,
cooper for the colony. He was immortalized in
Longfellow's poem "The Courtship of Myles
Standish," which is known to most schoolchildren.
A youth of twenty-one when he sailed to America,
John was fair of face and figure, a good talker, and
respected by all. He put his name on the Mayflower
Compact, and afterwards proved his worth, not
only at his craft, but in duties helpful to the plantation. He married Priscilla Mullins, whose parents
both died the first year. Their issue were more numerous than that of any other Pilgrim couple, for
he was a lusty young man. In turn he served as surveyor of highways, member of the council of war,
governor's assistant, and treasurer; later he was a
deputy from Duxbury. His craft of coopering was
important, inasmuch as all the Pilgrims' supplies
came packed in wooden barrels, with hoops of bent
ash. Later, at least on both ends, the hoops were
iron, in order to take the shock when dropped.

Alden died in 1687 at Duxbury. His wife had died
about 1650.

Edward Winslow

The Plymouth colony was blessed with some
men whose talents developed as the years went by.
One such man was Edward Winslow, a native of
Droitwich, England, born 18 October 1595. A
printer by trade, he was a member of the Leyden
congregation, and only twenty-five when the move
was made to America. He had faith enough to put
some money in the enterprise. At Cape Cod he was
a member of one of the exploring parties; later he
proved to be a good contact with the Indians, who
respected him. His first wife dying in 1621, Winslow married Susanna, widow of William White
and sister of Samuel Fuller, the Pilgrim physician.
When the ship *Fortune* arrived at the colony in
1622, Winslow sailed back to England, carrying
reports on the progress of the colony. Nearing
home, the ship was taken by a French privateer,
but Winslow was freed and got to England safely.
He returned to Plymouth, but sailed again the
following year to further negotiate with the Adventurers, and get more cash for supplies. On the
return voyage he took back to Plymouth three
heifers and a bull, the first livestock to reach the
colony. While on another visit to his homeland, he
published his own report on the colony. Winslow
was one of those who shouldered the Pilgrim debt;
in return he obtained trading concessions in Maine,
Cape Ann, Buzzards Bay, and, later, on the Connecticut River. He was able to build himself a fine
residence at Green Harbor with money obtained
through his trading ventures. Not content to stay
there, he made other voyages, dying in the West Indies on 8 May 1655. His was a useful and well-
spent life.

Stephen Hopkins

Hopkins took an active part in the affairs of the
colony, serving as assistant governor for several
years. He was both farmer and trader until his
death in 1644.

John Howland

John Howland was rescued at sea during the

Mayflower's voyage to America when a wave swept him overboard. To the Pilgrims, this was an example of God's grace, especially as Howland turned out to be a useful member of the colony. He was a member of Governor Carver's family, and may have been one of his heirs, since Carver had no children of his own. John was a member of the shallop crew that found Plymouth Harbor.

As the years went by, Howland served as an assistant and member of the governor's council. Later, he commanded the Pilgrim trading post at Kennebec, Maine. He died at Plymouth in 1672.

Samuel Fuller

A man who not only served the colony well, but helped save lives, was Samuel Fuller, the Pilgrims' physician. Fuller was a competent doctor, hampered only by the lack of accurate knowledge of the human body and the false medical theories of his day (see chapter 7). Fuller had settled in Leyden in 1609, and may have studied at the university there. He was twice married and twice bereaved before taking a third wife, Bridget. She did not sail on the *Mayflower,* but arrived on the *Ann* in 1623, and survived until sometime after March 1664, when

the family was living at Rehoboth. Fuller served not only the Pilgrim colony at Plymouth, but was called to Salem and Boston to help cope with epidemics. Fuller raised several children by Bridget and his previous wives. He died at the age of seventy-one, in Middleboro, Massachusetts.

In mentioning the more prominent Pilgrims, and their service to the colony, we do not imply that they alone were responsible for its success. There were those whose manual skills contributed to the actual building of dwellings, storehouses, and fortifications, but we have no record of the trades represented at Plymouth. We do know that Francis Eaton was a carpenter, and John Alden may have been able to work in this trade, in addition to his coopering. Eaton possibly acted as a foreman, helping others to construct their own houses, especially when complicated joints had to be made in the timbers of the house framework. There had to be a blacksmith among the colonists, for making nails, hinges, and a wide variety of iron tools; he also had to repair broken tools. When a house needed a roof, there were those who knew what reeds to cut for thatch, and how to apply it to keep out the weather. We shall cover all the activities of colony building in greater detail in later chapters.

Chapter 3

The Mayflower Crossing

JOHN CARVER and Robert Cushman, the agents chosen by the Pilgrims to secure financing and supplies for their colony in America, found that they had a lot of persuading to do. They went first to the London Company to ask for a patent and backing for a colony in its territory, but they met opposition; the company, having had reverses in its dealings with the Jamestown colony, was reluctant to back others in a similar venture, nor was it sure of its position with regard to a group of dissenters. It so happened that at this time two of the Pilgrim leaders had made themselves subject to arrest by publishing and distributing tracts offensive to the crown and church. This did not help the Pilgrims in their search for backing, and the Leyden congregation began to despair of obtaining any. However, a minor London merchant, Thomas Weston, had as his agent in Holland Edward Pickering, who was married to one of the Pilgrim women. Through Pickering, Weston may have heard that the Dutch authorities had offered backing through the Dutch West India Company, if the Pilgrims would settle in Dutch territory in the New World. But the Pilgrims felt that they should cut off ties with the Dutch, and thus Dutch influence on their young. Hearing of this, Weston offered to back them, along with other merchants eager to risk capital in a foreign venture.

THE PILGRIMS' AGREEMENT WITH THE LONDON ADVENTURERS

Cushman negotiated a deal with these so-called London Adventurers, based on the agreement made with the Virginia colonists by the London Company. John Pierce, one of the merchants associated with Weston, had a patent from this company, and he persuaded the Leyden group to make use of it. To this they agreed, under the following terms. Three groups were set up: (1) adventurers in England (seventy in all) at ten pounds per share, (2) adventurer-planters, given two shares for each ten pounds in consideration of their settling, and (3) planters, given one share each for their labor. Both capital and profits were to belong to a joint stock for seven years, at the end of which period they were to be divided proportionately. Whether Cushman secretly negotiated a further deal or not, the final terms were harsher than those originally agreed to. In consequence, there was much hard feeling aroused, since there was not enough money raised to complete the final deals, which entailed the chartering and provisioning of a ship to take the Pilgrims to their colony in America.

TROUBLES WITH THE *SPEEDWELL*

While arrangements were being made for the voyage in England, the Leyden congregation sold off their possessions to buy the fifty-ton *Speedwell*, a small vessel they intended to use in the colony for fishing and trading. With Brewster as leader, the group sailed for England on 22 July 1620, only to find on arrival that there were financial difficulties, with outstanding bills holding up the sailing of the chartered ship *Mayflower*; some of the original backers pulled out at the last minute. The die being now cast, there was nothing to do but sell some of their supplies to get out of debt, a move which was to cause near-starvation in the months ahead. It was August before they sailed. This meant they would be at sea during the stormy season. Several false starts were made by the two ships, and each time it was the *Speedwell* which was in trouble. She was a leaking, overmasted ship which they abandoned in the end, making necessary the crowding of her passengers onto the *Mayflower*. Some were too discouraged to undertake the trip, and stayed behind. Even so, there were 102 passengers, officers, and crew aboard the *Mayflower*. Some of those who sailed, including Myles Standish, their chosen military leader, and the fourteen indentured

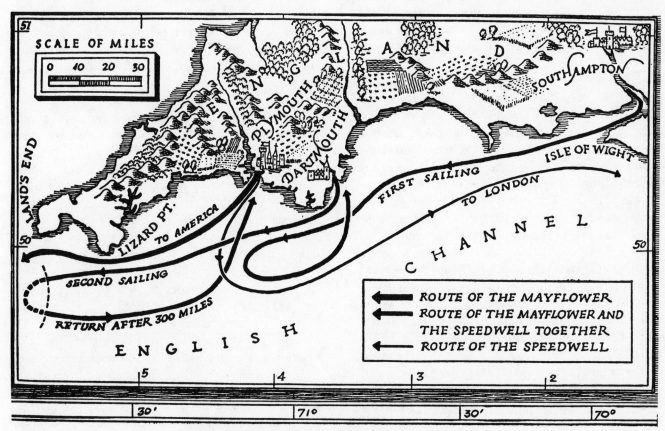

FALSE STARTS OF THE *MAYFLOWER* AND *SPEEDWELL*

The map shows the abortive sailings of the ships *Mayflower* and *Speedwell*, the result of the latter vessel's unseaworthiness.

servants and hired artisans, were not Pilgrims. Thirty-five were members of the Leyden congregation; they constituted the "Saints." The remaining Pilgrims were from Southampton, London, and elsewhere, and were known as "Strangers."

SAILING VESSELS IN THE SEVENTEENTH CENTURY

To cross the Altantic in those days was never a pleasure trip and, under the conditions prevailing, the voyage of the *Mayflower* must have been a ghastly experience. To get an accurate picture of the kind of ship used to transport the Pilgrims to the New World in 1620, let us trace the development of sailing vessels, which resulted from the many voyages made under the sponsorship of Prince Henry of Portugal. These voyages proved the need for larger ships with better sail plans, and these Henry had built in his own shipyards. As a result, a type of ship resulted which had a larger and more capacious hull, complete with three masts, on two of which were fitted square sails affixed to yards rigged athwartship; the mizzenmast carried a lateen sail on a long spar rigged fore and aft. On the bowsprit, another square sail was hung. This, in conjunction with the mizzensail, helped to balance the ship and aid in steering; neither had much driving power when the ship sailed before the wind. Such ships were useful on long voyages, but most captains took along one or more pinnaces, which remained lateen-rigged. Such ships were useful for inshore exploration and trading, and as auxiliary vessels. Columbus returned from his first voyage on such a ship, after his flag-ship *Santa Maria* was wrecked on the shore of Hispaniola.

By the time the Pilgrims were ready to sail to the New World, these three-masted ships were common, and were built in several sizes for a variety of uses. The *Mayflower*, on which the Pilgrims sailed under the command of Captain Christopher Jones, was a fairly small merchant ship whose voyages are documented in port logs. She was, for the most part, engaged in the wine trade between France and England, in consequence of which she was known as a 'sweet' ship, her bilges being free from the residues of noisome cargoes.

Unfortunately, there are no known plans of the *Mayflower* extant, but marine scholars, naval ar-

chitectural historians, and sea-diver archaeologists have unearthed documents, and even actual wrecks, from which they have been able to formulate plans. In some instances, models or full-size replicas have been built from them, as witness the ship *Mayflower II*, designed by American naval achitect William A. Baker, and built in England. The vessel is now on public exhibition at the State Pier in Plymouth, Massachusetts, having been sailed to America by Captain Alan Villiers and crew in 1957. In other countries there are original ships preserved in museums, from Viking longboats to a Swedish warship, the *Vasa*, raised almost intact from the bottom of Stockholm Harbor, complete with armament and a variety of seventeenth-century artifacts. Other wrecks, many of which have been looted or their contents dispersed by ocean currents, have been located by divers.

THE *MAYFLOWER II*

Lacking original plans of the *Mayflower*, we must be content with Baker's plans for the *Mayflower II*, based on research by Baker and Dr. R. C. Anderson of Greenwich, England, concerning sixteenth-century merchant ships. Specifications are as follows:

Length—104 feet; Beam (widest part amidships)—25-1/2 feet; Draft—13 feet; Burden—181 tons.

The ship has two decks, and a half-deck atop which is a small cabin for the captain. Clearance between decks is six feet. Under the half-deck are the great cabin and the steerage; the latter, as the name suggests, is the station for the steersman, who, by means of a whipstaff attached to the tiller, controls the ship's rudder to steer the ship. In the forward part of the ship is the forecastle, a small cabin designated as crew's quarters, and used for cooking, eating, and sleeping. Forward of this is the beakhead, through which the bowsprit protrudes over the stem of the ship. To keep the ship on an even keel, and to counteract the pressure of the sails, a ballast of stone is placed over the keelson and between the ribs, in an area known as the bilge, below the cargo deck.

The two masts and bowsprit are equipped with

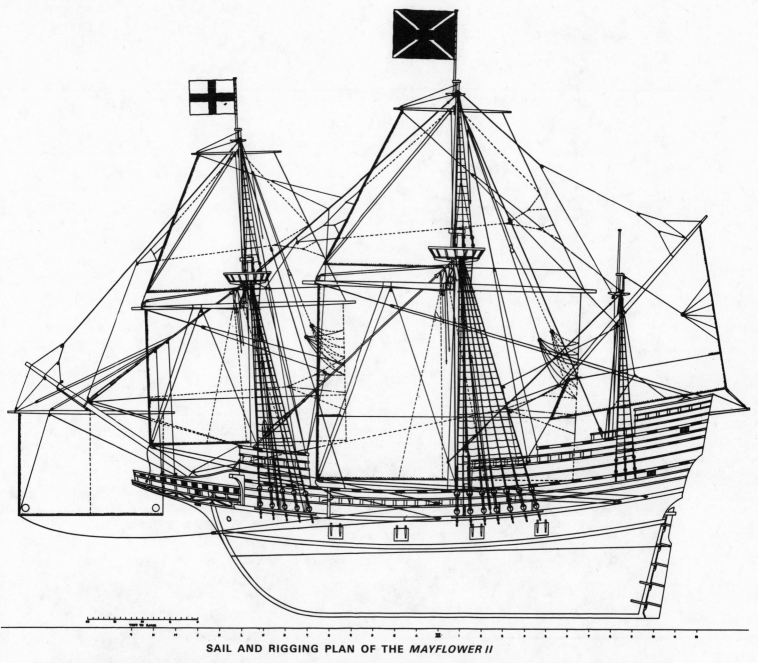

SAIL AND RIGGING PLAN OF THE *MAYFLOWER II*

The flag on the foremast has the cross of Saint George; the mainmast carries the Union Jack of the seventeenth century. The beakhead, from which the spritsail mast protrudes (at the bow), was the place designated for the performance of bodily functions.—*Plan copyright © 1958 by William A. Baker*

yards, carried athwartship (at right angles to the keel), onto which sails are fastened. The mizzenmast has the yard rigged fore and aft. Heights of the masts are as follows:

Mainmast—67-1/2 feet, with a topmast of 33 feet 9 inches. Foremast—57 feet 9 inches, with a topmast of 29 feet. (These topmasts rise from tublike structures called tops; formerly defensive positions for bowmen or musketeers, they presently serve as lookout positions for the better sighting of land and for handling the topsails.)

Mizzenmast—41 feet 8 inches high, with a fore-and-aft-positioned yard 30 feet 4-1/2 inches long.

SCALE MODEL OF THE BARK *MAYFLOWER II*

Mainmast and foremast are each fitted with two yards, to which sails are fixed. The yards slide up and down the mast on parrels, wooden rollers threaded on a line, making for easier hoisting and lowering. The sails have no reef points with which to shorten sail in a blow. They can be increased in area by the fitting of bonnets on their lower edge. Taking off bonnets in strong winds is the equivalent of reefing to reduce sail area. The spritsail and lateen have little driving power in following winds, but they do aid in balancing the ship, making steering easier. Total sail area is 5,065 square feet.

THE BARK *MAYFLOWER II* UNDER SAIL

This replica of a sixteenth-century merchant vessel was designed by American naval architect William A. Baker, and was built in Upham's boatyard, Brixham, England. It sailed to America in 1957, under the command of Captain Alan Villiers, with a British crew.—*Photograph courtesy of The Dicksons, Plymouth, Massachusetts*

STERN VIEW OF THE *MAYFLOWER II*

Note the mayflower (hawthorn blossom), after which the ship was named, above the windows of the great cabin. The wide belly of the ship at the waterline provided space on the deck below and for cargo carried beneath it.—*Photograph courtesy of The Dicksons, Plymouth, Massachusetts*

STEERING WITH THE WHIPSTAFF

The whipstaff was connected to the tiller below, which actuated the rudder to steer the ship. Sailing orders were given to the steersman by an officer stationed on the deck above. The original *Mayflower* was steered in this fashion.

The previously mentioned whipstaff was an efficient steering device, remaining unchanged for centuries until the advent of the wheel for controlling the rudder. The steersman stood behind the whipstaff, receiving his orders from the mate on watch above and keeping his eyes on the compass in front of him. At night the compass was illuminated by so-called binnacle lights (oil lamps); the binnacle was the fixture in which the compass case was housed.

THE COMPASS

The compass in use in the seventeenth century had developed from a crude instrument consisting of a bowl of water on which floated a magnetized needle pushed through a sliver of wood. The needle, magnetized with a lode stone (magnetic rock), pointed roughly north. A later type had a compass card on which was drawn a compass rose, marked off with the cardinal points and with a fleur-de-lis indicating north. This card, on which was pivoted a compass needle, floated on water (or spirits, if the ship was sailing in a cold climate). The bowl was sealed with a glass cover, and was suspended in gimbals, two rings, the outer fixed to the compass case, the inner pivoted in the outer ring. By this means the compass was kept comparatively steady when the ship heaved and rolled. A modern small boat compass is marked with the cardinal points and degrees. Its card is floated in alcohol, and the bowl is fitted in gimbals; but it differs very little from the one used aboard the *Mayflower* in 1620.

The compass needle points only roughly north. Early mariners found their compass needle behaving in an erratic manner on certain courses in different locations, particularly in the area of Hudson Bay, near which the north magnetic pole is located. The difference between true and magnetic north is called variation, and mariners had to work out tables of correction when plotting a compass course. Another compass error could be caused by the presence of any iron in the vicinity of the compass. To correct for this the navigator had to "box the compass" by sailing his ship on various courses, noting the compass deviation on each run, and then working out the errors noted. To correct such deviation, the steersman could place some iron object

near enough to the compass to bring the needle to the correct position.

The modern compass rose is graduated from 0 clockwise to 360 degrees, a degree being 60 geographical miles. This estimate was arrived at in 1756. Before this, mariners had based their estimate of a degree on the calculations of Eratosthenes (third century B.C.), or Poseidonius (first century B.C.). English seamen based their estimate on the latter. They allotted 5,000 feet to the mile, 3 miles to the league, and 20 leagues to a degree. Spanish and Portuguese navigators used the measure of 17.5 leagues to a degree. Nevertheless, most navigators found their way with surprising accuracy, returning to known destinations repeatedly by working out their course from their marked charts.

"SHOOTING THE SUN"

A navigator needed more than a compass to find his way over the sea. He had to have some means of finding his position, and to do this he "shot the sun," or a known star, to find the angle of a celestial body in relation to the horizon. From this reading he determined his latitude. To fix his longitude was beyond him, except by dead reckoning. Nevertheless, it was not just by luck that navigators reached their destination. Columbus was able to find his way back to the islands he discovered, and sailors who followed after him made ports to which they were headed, finding their way back home without trouble. Accurate determination of longitude was made possible by John Harrison's invention of a reliable sea chronometer in 1761. Soon afterwards most ships carried such a clock, making their navigation much easier.

Columbus is said to have carried an astrolabe for taking sun sights, but he may also have carried a quadrant. Both these instruments were useful, but hard to use on a tossing ship, the astrolabe in particular. An Englishman, John Davis, invented a better device called a cross-staff, a wooden staff with a sliding crosspiece. In use, the eye was positioned at the end of the staff, which was pointed towards the sun, the crosspiece being then slid until its top edge was just under the sun. The angle between sun and horizon could then be read on the staff, which was graduated along its length. Davis improved on this method by inventing the backstaff,

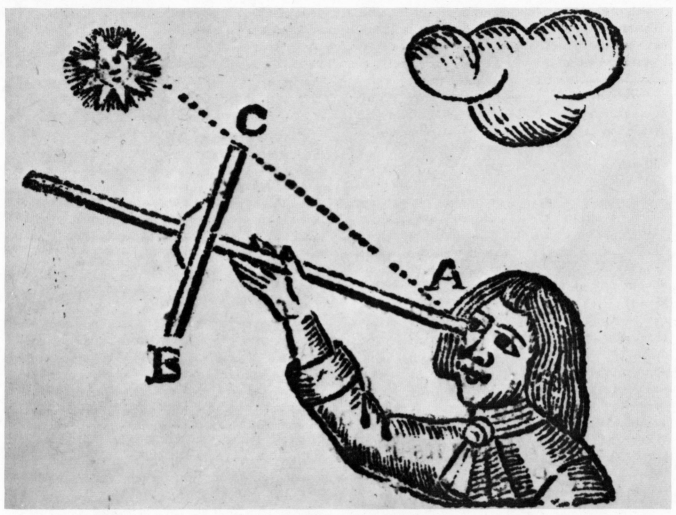

"SHOOTING THE SUN"

The instrument shown is a cross-staff, a navigating device such as would have been used by Captain Jones aboard the *May-flower.*

which obviated looking directly at the sun, sighting being done with one's back to it. This instrument lasted into the early nineteenth century, when the octant came into use, followed by the sextant, which is still used today.

DUTIES OF SHIPS' OFFICERS AND MEN

Navigational duties on a ship of the seventeenth century were delegated to the ship's master, although the captain might be consulted in case of doubt, or to check sights taken in stormy weather;

two sights taken by two individuals could then be compared. The master and his mates ran the ship, together with the boatswain (bos'n), who had charge of the seamen. The ship's company stood watches, usually of four-hour duration, with each man having a given station or duty. The more intelligent sailors were petty officers, capable of steering the ship under the direction of the mate on watch.

It was important when at sea that all orders be understood and acted upon at once. For this reason, all parts of the ship were named—fore, aft, amidships, starboard, and larboard (port). Starboard denoted the right side of the ship looking forward, and larboard the left side. On an order to go aloft, certain crew members climbed up the shrouds, which were "rattled down," crossropes forming steps. In stormy weather all hands might go aloft to take in sails in a hurry.

Men went to sea for a variety of reasons, but those who made the sea their profession were capable seamen, many having served with the fishing fleets that regularly sailed to the Grand Bank off Newfoundland. It took skill to know and handle the many lines aboard a ship, and courage to go aloft in all weathers to set or take in sails.

Daily navigational routine called for taking sights to fix position, and the heaving of the chip-log to gauge the speed of the ship through the water. The log consisted of a length of log-line attached at one end to a chip-log of lead-weighted wood, a reel to unwind the log-line from, and a minute or half-minute sandglass. Casting the log over the stern and measuring the length of the line paid out in a minute, multiplied by sixty, gave the distance sailed in one hour. This could be converted from feet into fathoms into miles per hour. The knots tied into the log-line gave rise to the term knot (knots per hour), in use to this day.

In conjunction with the log-line, a device called a log-board was used. On this was recorded the ship's course and speed. Every twenty-four hours this information was transferred to a logbook, and the board cleared for the next day's run.

To get from one point to another the navigator planned a great-circle course. This, if marked on a globe, formed a circle, the shortest distance from point to point. This could only be done if the point of destination was known. In practice such a route was not followed, the navigator taking advantage of driving winds, making note of his course sailed, and working back to his circle route when possible. Courses were plotted from rhumb lines marked on his chart.

Using a pair of dividers, he stepped off his course in relation to one of these lines, and followed it as winds permitted.

Some members of the ship's crew were specialists, practicing a craft or skill necessary for the ship's well-being. The carpenter took care of keeping the ship in repair, especially any part damaged at sea. The sailmaker kept all sails in repair, or made new ones if necessary. The cook and his helpers prepared hot meals when possible, or handed out cold rations in stormy weather, when it was impossible to have a fire in his stove. If livestock was carried for food on the voyage, the cook killed and dressed it, salting any surplus for future use. A steward disbursed food from stock to the cook, and helped serve the meals. He issued grog (rum and water) if ordered to do so by the captain. Water, spirits, and dry goods were stored aboard in barrels, the cooper seeing that these containers were kept intact during the voyage. The Pilgrims took along John Alden as their cooper, and he may well have been kept busy on that stormy voyage of 1620, since barrels were then hooped with wooden, rather than iron rings. Such hoops had to be kept tight to keep the barrel-staves snug.

To counteract the pressure of wind on the sails, a ship had to be weighted with stone ballast, placed over the keelson and ribs of the ship in the bilge beneath the cargo deck. On a long voyage the cargo was a form of ballast, and its weight had to be evenly distributed to keep the ship on an even keel. During rough weather the bilge was apt to accumulate seawater, which had to be pumped out daily, or more frequently at times. This was done with the aid of wooden pumps, which ran from the bilge up to the main deck. Suction was obtained with leather washers and check valve. If the bilges were fouled with debris, sailors were sent below to clear the valves. This could be an unpleasant task if latrine buckets had been emptied aboard, instead of overboard. Such a task was performed by the lowest-rated seamen.

When a ship was nearing land, the master liked to know the nature of the seabed beneath his ship. This told him several things, including depth of water, his approximate relation to the ocean shelf, and whether the bottom afforded good anchorage in case of need. To determine all these facts he used a dipsie (deep sea) lead and line. There were two types used, one having a fourteen-pound lead and another with a seven-pound lead. The ends of each were hollow and filled with tallow, which would pick up samples of the bottom. The sounding lines were marked off in certain fathom (six feet) lengths, indicated by tags of material of different colors or textures known as "marks." A fathom length without a mark was known as a "deep."

PLOTTING THE *MAYFLOWER'S* COURSE

Captain Jones is shown plotting his course on a chart, aided by tables published for seamen of the seventeenth century, in a diorama at Plimoth Plantation.

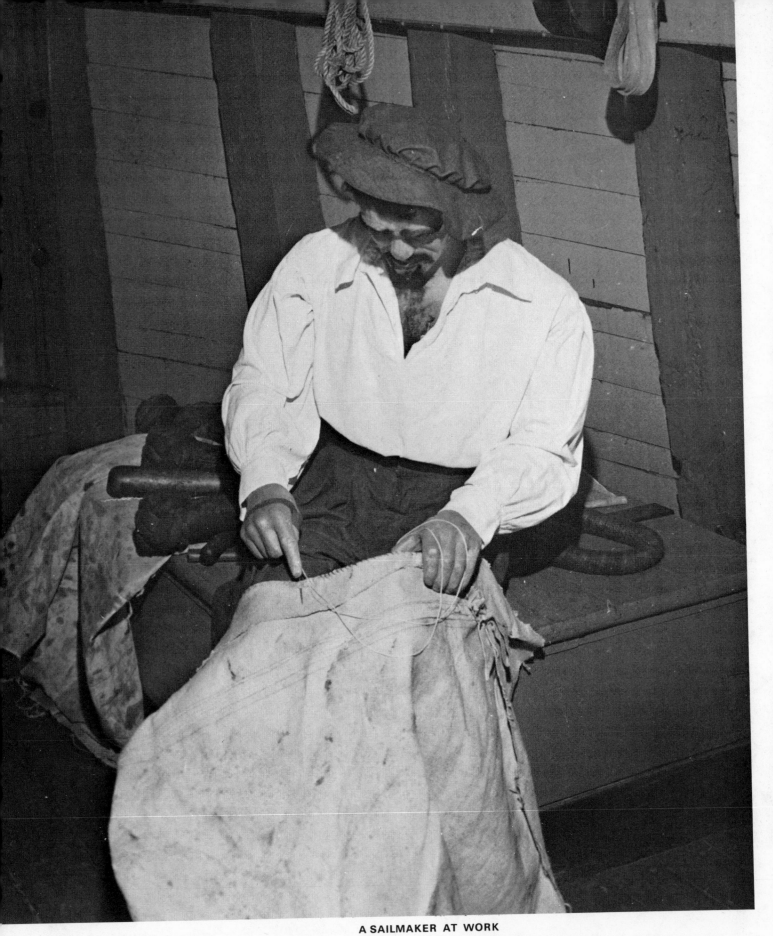

A SAILMAKER AT WORK

This scene shows a sailmaker repairing a sail aboard the *Mayflower*.

PREPARING A MEAL IN THE GALLEY OF THE *MAYFLOWER*

Depicted here are the cook and his helper. On seventeenth-century ships it was customary to build a brick fireplace in the galley with an opening in the roof to let out the smoke. Such a fireplace could be used only in reasonably calm weather. To the right of the cook is an opened cask of salted meat.

CUTAWAY DRAWING OF THE *MAYFLOWER II*

Note the crowded conditions aboard and how the cargo is stowed. The captain, high on the poop deck (left top), is shown "shooting the sun" to determine his position at sea.—*Drawing courtesy of The Dicksons, Plymouth, Massachusetts*

SHIPBOARD SANITARY AND COOKING FACILITIES

Life aboard a ship of the seventeenth century was uncomfortable for all, especially during the cold months, there being no way of heating the ship. Clothing was kept on for the duration of the voyage, even at night. There were no toilet facilities aboard, making the use of latrine buckets necessary. The beakhead, usually designated as the place to perform bodily functions, was awash for most of the voyage, except in calm weather. To prepare meals under stormy circumstances was difficult, no fires being possible below deck, unless a charcoal brazier could be lighted; even then, smoke made this inadvisable. These conditions contributed to the sickness which afflicted many of the passengers aboard the *Mayflower*; dampness, cold, and lack of proper food took their toll. One man died, and one barely escaped death when swept overboard. This was John Howland, who had the luck to catch hold of a trailing halliard, with which the crew hauled him back aboard.

SHIPBOARD CLOTHING

The clothing worn by the passengers was of wool, or a mixture of linen and wool. Males wore knee-length pants, cut full, and fastened at a point below the knees. A linen shirt was worn, over which a coat or jerkin was added, the latter often made of leather. Collars and cuffs were of linen. Most wore wool stockings, sometimes without a full foot. Shoes were the pull-on type, with leather ties. Hats were of felt, with wide brim. Sometimes woolen caps, or Monmouth caps which could be pulled over the ears in cold weather, were worn. Both men and women wore large hats, the women having a linen cap over their hair, and sometimes a binding which fastened under the chin. Capes were in common use by both sexes. Children wore clothing similar to their elders'.

Under the crowded conditions aboard the *Mayflower*, much movement was not possible; so people lived, ate, and slept in an allotted space. Perhaps this closeness contributed to warmth, but it was most unhealthy. It was impossible to keep dry, with

CREWMAN'S HAMMOCK ABOARD THE *MAYFLOWER*

This hammock is forward on the 'tween deck. The hammock, brought back from the Caribbean by Columbus, was used on ships until the twentieth century.

SHIPBOARD COOKING WITH A CHARCOAL BRAZIER

Pilgrim girls aboard the *Mayflower* are shown cooking a meal over a charcoal brazier, which could only be done in relatively calm weather.

seawater seeping through cracks in the sloping sides of the ship. Decks were reasonably tight, being kept wet by the seas breaking over them. So, wet and cold for most of the voyage, half of the passengers died during the first months ashore in the New England winter. Their misery notwithstanding, none of the passengers elected to return to England on the *Mayflower*, preferring life ashore to the misery of another trans-Atlantic crossing.

SHIPBOARD MEDICINE

Although the *Mayflower* carried both a surgeon and a doctor, we know little about their treatment

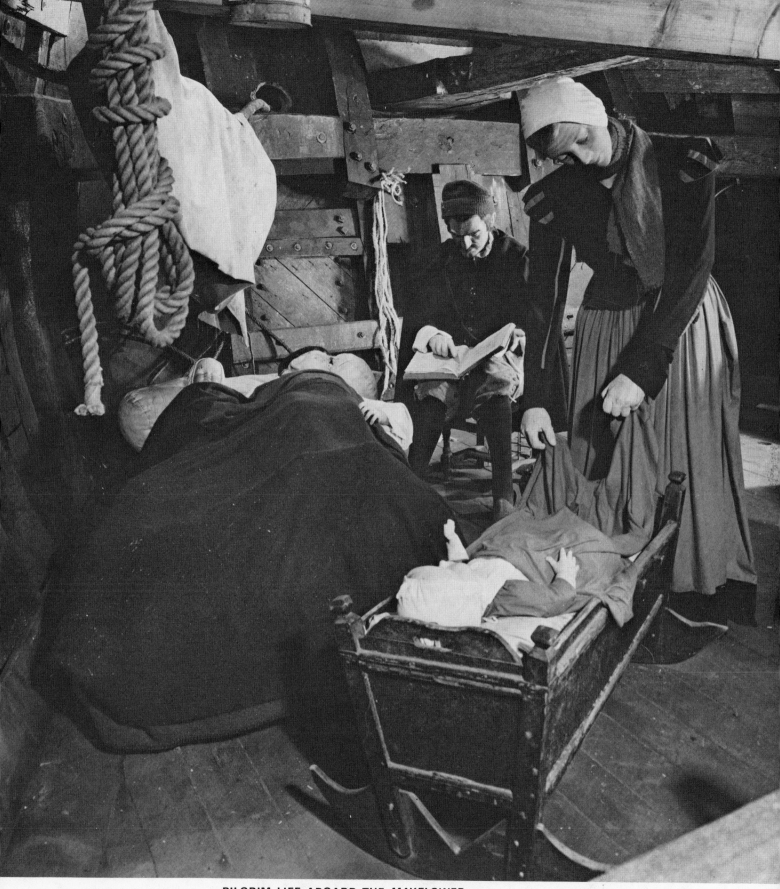

PILGRIM LIFE ABOARD THE *MAYFLOWER*

In the foreground a mother puts her baby to sleep beside a bed on which a boy is sleeping. In the background a Pilgrim sits reading his Bible.

of the sick aboard the ship. Not much is known about Giles Heale, the surgeon, but fellow physician Samuel Fuller did prove his worth, not only at Plymouth, but later in the Bay Colony.

SHIPS' ARMAMENT

The presence of Spanish treasure ships in the waters of the Altantic attracted pirate ships, such as those of Drake. They did not hesitate to prey on any ship flying an alien flag. In consequence, most ships were armed, and the *Mayflower* was no exception. She carried cannon on her 'tween-deck, along with smaller arms to repel boarders. The *Mayflower's* armament was more than sufficient to her needs, and the captain left behind armament enough for the use of the Pilgrims. This they mounted on the deck of their fort, built some time after they had built their houses. It was fortunate that the Pilgrim ships met no pirates during its crossing, few such vessels wishing to frequent those stormy waters at that time of year.

One incident that occurred during the voyage caused some alarm. A great sea caused one of the main deckbeams to crack. Fortunately, among the Pilgrim possessions was a "greate iron screwe" of unknown purpose. This was used as a jack to force the beam back into place while a support was placed beneath it. There are no reports that this beam gave any further trouble, the *Mayflower* completing a return voyage without further incident.

A SHALLOP UNDER SAIL

Note the portside leeboard. This was lowered when the boat came about on the other tack. The foresail is a jib. The mainsail is hoisted on a sprit, or long boom, which may be secured to the mast to make room for men fishing. Besides fishing, this double-ended craft was used as a workboat, for setting out and retrieving anchors, and as a coastal vessel. A windlass was placed in the stern for use in raising anchors. A shallop had places for from five to ten oars a side, depending on its length. Shallops were usually under thirty feet long, with a beam of six feet.

The Pilgrims made good use of their several shallops—the one brought over knocked down aboard the *Mayflower* and others built subsequently as the Plymouth colony expanded. The shallop moored next to the *Mayflower II* at the State Pier in Plymouth, Massachusetts was designed by William A. Baker for Plimoth Plantation and built at Plymouth Boatyard.—*Drawing by William A. Baker*

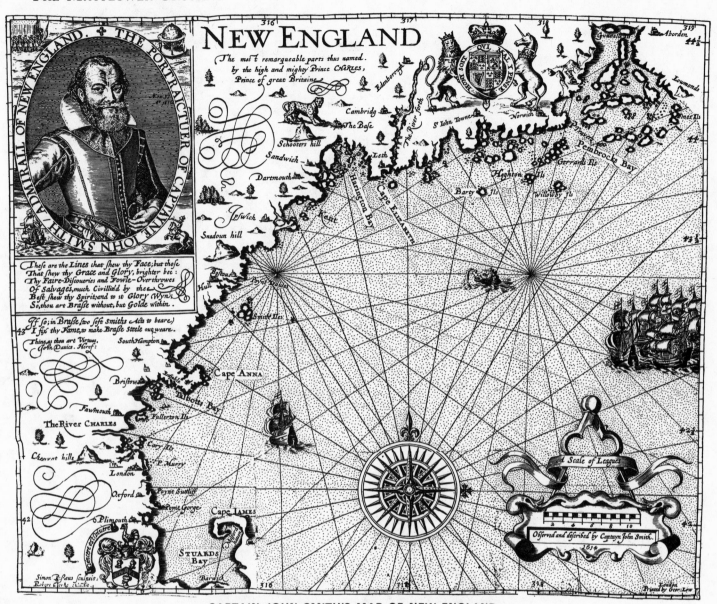

CAPTAIN JOHN SMITH'S MAP OF NEW ENGLAND—
Reproduced from the Pequot Collection, Yale University Library

AUXILIARY VESSELS

In addition to their flagship, early voyagers often took along a smaller vessel, usually a pinnace, as an auxiliary for use inshore on exploratory trips, or for trading along a coast. Such ships were usually rigged with fore-and-aft lateen sails or spritsails, which were more efficient when sailing against the wind. The Pilgrims had intended their *Speedwell* to serve this purpose but, after abandoning her, they were left with their shallop, which they shipped partly knocked down aboard the *Mayflower*.

THE PILGRIMS' LANDING AT PLYMOUTH

It was nine weeks before land was sighted. This was Cape Cod, seeing which, Captain Jones turned his ship southwards towards Virginia. Running into difficulties off the coast, he decided to turn back and find a safe harbor, for all were weary. He set his course north, sailing around the tip of Cape Cod, where he anchored the ship inside a large bay (Provincetown) on 11 November. Once the ship was at rest the passengers crowded on deck, and the

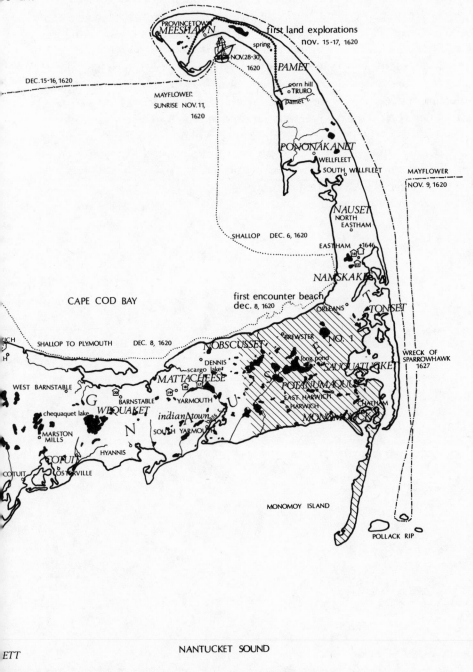
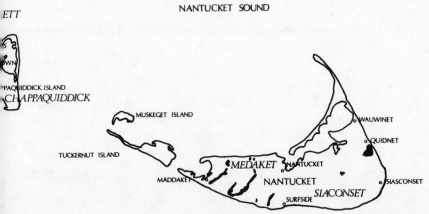

religious among them knelt down and prayed to God for their deliverance. They were safe, but far from established; their patent for Virginia was not valid here, and they had no government of their own. It was at this point that their leaders drew up the Mayflower Compact, under which they would create officers and make their own laws for self-government. John Carver was elected as their governor for one year.

While the ship lay at anchor, exploring parties went ashore to seek a site, while others sailed their quickly reassembled shallop farther down the coast to look for a safer harbor and site. The shallop returned with the news of a sheltered harbor and suitable colony site. This was at Plymouth, which was so named by Captain John Smith on his map of 1614, a copy of which the Pilgrims had in their possession. Compared to the Cape Cod site, Plymouth was ideal, inasmuch as there was cleared land there, with a brook affording a good water supply. Captain Jones sailed his ship to Plymouth, but could not anchor close to shore; his ship, however was protected from the sea by a long spit of land (Plymouth beach). Safe though the Pilgrims were in this location, the worst was yet to come. Winter was no time in which to establish a colony, since no crops could be planted until spring and, as we have seen, their supplies had been depleted to pay their bills. But here they were, and they made the best of things.

Chapter 4

Village Life of the Pilgrims

As the *Mayflower* eased into her anchorage in Plymouth Bay, her maindeck must have been filled with passengers, eager for a look at the new land that was to be their home. The scene before them could not have gladdened their hearts. What trees they could see were bare of leaves, standing gaunt in the distant forest. The foreground was filled with the stumps of burned trees, relics of the Indian method of slash-and-burn agriculture. It may have been this lack of ground cover that made game scarce, thus contributing to the starvation the Pilgrims would suffer when their supplies ran low.

Nevertheless, the choice of Plymouth as a colony site was far better than the swampy, fever-ridden environs of Jamestown. The Pilgrim site, as we know from the accounts of Bradford and others, was on a slope rising from the sea. Such a location, high enough for a good view out to sea, lent itself to the building of a fort. Beside the hill ran a stream, a good water supply and a place to moor a shallop.

EARLY ACCOUNTS OF NEW ENGLAND

It must be remembered that most of the Pilgrims were city-bred, or from towns and villages in a civilized country, and few were fitted for the life of a frontiersman. Only a few were familiar with the tasks of a farmer, and the humbler crafts some had practiced in Holland would be of little use to them in combating the wilderness. Had the Pilgrims been better equipped, and more familiar with the land, or had they read some of the glowing accounts written about New England by former voyagers who knew the land well, they might have faced their tasks with more assurance. Captain John Smith was one such writer. Smith, an ardent exponent of colonization in New England, never was given the opportunity to develop his sound ideas. He saw New England prospering from fishing, shipbuilding, and the manufacture of naval stores from gums and tars furnished by the abundant pine forests. Smith called New England "A Countrie to affright, then delight one." In Smith's words, "The sea there is the strangest fishpond I ever saw; and the barren isles so furnished with good woods, springs, fruits, fish, and fowle, that it makes me think that though the coast is rockie, the interior parts may well (notwithstanding) be fertile." Smith's opinions may have been made known to the Pilgrims at the time he sought to be their leader.

For another favorable account of New England by a contemporary of the Pilgrims let us turn to Thomas Morton's *The New English Canaan,* published in Holland in 1637. We chose his writing because, although accounted a scoundrel by the Pilgrims for his dubious dealings with the Indians (see chapter 10), he was a romantic, with the soul of a poet. In his dedication of the book to the king of England he called New England "the modell of a Rich, hopefull and very beautiful Country worthy of the Title of Nature's Masterpiece." He gave credit to God for visiting upon the Indians a disease which almost wiped them out, thus making the land safer for Englishmen to live in. Morton was a believer in Aristotle's theory of five zones of the world, two only of which were habitable, and New England was in one of them, being a "Zona Temperata" in the "golden meane." Futhermore, said he, ships were not attacked by worms in New England harbors. In this he was correct, the wood-boring teredo inhabiting only tropical waters. Morton was no naturalist, wrongly naming rocks, plants, and animals, as he compared them with those he was familiar with in England. In his book Morton included much information about the ways of Indians: how they cultivated their crops, what foods they ate and how they were cooked, and what animals they hunted, and for what purpose. Morton's poetic bent is revealed in the following description of the New England landscape: "goodly groves of trees, rounded hillocks, delicate faire large plaines, sweet cristall fountains, and clear running streames that twine in fine meanders through the meads . . . fowles in abundance, fish in multitude; and I discovered besides, Millions of Turtledoves. . . pecking of the full ripe pleasant grapes that were supported by lusty trees, whose fruitfull loade did cause the armes to bend . . . for in mine eie t'was Nature's Masterpiece . . . . if this land be not rich, then is the whole world poore." And he was right; New England still is a beautiful region.

PUBLIC AND PRIVATE BUILDINGS

Among the bounties of nature which the Pilgrims found at Plymouth was a plentiful supply of timber for building. This advantage, however, was considerably diminished by the weather, with frost in the ground, and alternate days of rain, snow, and sleet. From all accounts, the winter of 1620 was not severe; had it been, it is doubtful if any would have survived. As it was, half of the passengers from the *Mayflower* died in the first few months, mostly from a sickness the true nature of which is not known, although there are many medical theories as to its nature.

The first building to go up was a common house, which was almost finished, except for the roof, in three weeks' time. Its size was twenty feet square. It was constructed to hold supplies from the ship, but, instead, first served as a house for those without family, then as a temporary hospital during those days when half the passengers from the *Mayflower* died, together with five of her crew. This circumstance alone delayed housebuilding, those remaining fit having to take care of the sick and the burying of the dead. During the time the sick occupied the common house, there was a fire in its roof caused by a spark from the chimney igniting the underside of the thatch. Fortunately, not too much damage was done. When all the houses were built, the common house and others like it housed the Pilgrims' stores.

Despite all they suffered once ashore and on their own, the colonists managed to build several houses. Stephen Hopkins's house was erected before 16 January 1621, but we have no progress report on others, except a letter written to England, dated 11 December 1621, which mentions that seven houses had been erected, and four (possibly storehouses) for the use of the plantation. Mention was made of others for which material was being prepared.

Bradford, in his journal, made a rough sketch of the village layout, showing a street leading up the hill to the top, where a fort was to be built, along with a tall watchtower. Halfway up the hill was a cross-street and, to enfilade the crossroads, a small platform was to be set up, with four patereros (called "murtherers"), one at each corner. Choice of lots was by a drawing of straws or the like, large families being allotted more space than smaller units. Because of deaths, many families had no

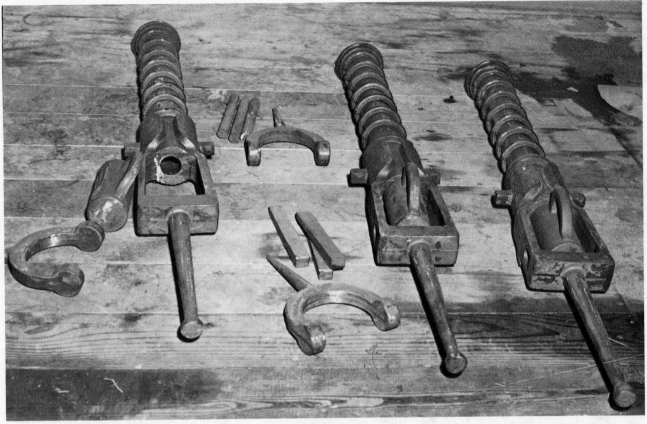

PATEREROS

The paterero, a breech-loading cannon with tapered bore, was an antipersonnel weapon shooting small shot, stones, or old iron. It was dangerous at close range. Shown here are cast iron reproductions made for Plimoth Plantation. In use this gun was mounted on a stout wooden pedestal.

blood ties, children and unmarried being placed as was deemed advisable. To every person was allotted half a pole (1 pole equalled 16-1/2 feet) in breadth, and three in length. When the houses were built, the village was to be enclosed with a palisade.

Fort and Palisade

In the summer of 1622 the fort-meetinghouse was erected and the palisade finished. Standish, who was a professional soldier, may have designed the fort in the manner of forts he had seen in Europe. It had to be strongly built to support the several cannon that were mounted on its upper deck. Bradford refers to "battlements" surrounding this deck which may have resembled those on castles but more likely were pointed boards, mentioned as being on the second fort built to replace the first circa 1634-35. One visitor to Plymouth estimated the completed palisade to be 10 feet high; another said it was 8 feet or thereabouts, and 2,700 feet in compass. It had three gates, one at each end of the cross-street and the other at the end opposite to the fort. In the manner of the day, this fence consisted of pointed posts driven in the earth, suitably braced, and with gun platforms set so as to rake with shot any attempting to climb over.

When the colony acquired livestock in 1642, it is likely that a barn was built, although no mention is made of such by Bradford or others. For housing animals and chickens there may have been rough sheds built, with corrals made of wattle to confine the flocks.

DE RASIERES' ACCOUNT OF THE PILGRIM VILLAGE

For a somewhat fuller account of the Pilgrim

THE FORT DECK AT PLIMOTH PLANTATION

The cannon in the foreground is a reproduction of a minion, which had a bore of 2.9 inches and shot a 3-1/2-inch iron ball. Simulated is the action of ramming rags or tow to retain the powder before inserting the iron ball. Behind the gun is a swab used to clean the barrel after firing. The gun mounted on the parapet is a base, a breechloader with a bore of 1-1/4 inches and a length of about 4-1/2 feet. It fired small shot. These guns are typical of those brought over on the *Mayflower*. A smaller cannon called a saker, with a 2.7-inch bore and firing a 2-3/4-inch ball, was also part of the Pilgrims' armament.

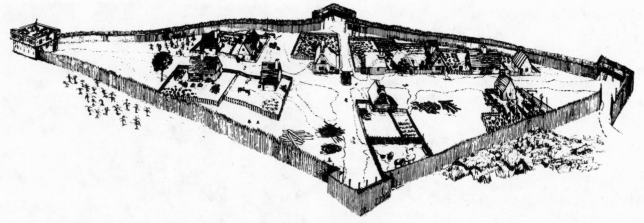

PALISADE AND FORT

This is a conjectural drawing of the Pilgrim village showing the fort and palisade enclosing the entire village. The houses all have garden plots. Crops were also grown outside the palisade on ground originally cleared by the Indians of that area.

PLIMOTH PLANTATION

This full-size reproduction of the Pilgrim village is located 3-1/2 miles from the center of Plymouth, Massachusetts. Note the sheep corral in the right foreground.

village than that provided by earlier visitors we must consult that furnished by Isaack de Rasieres, agent for the Dutch West India company and secretary to the governor of New Amsterdam. De Rasieres wrote of Plymouth, which he visited in 1627, when there was more to see. His description follows:

At the south side of the town there flows down a small river of fresh water very rapid, but shallow, which takes its rise from several lakes in the land above, and there empties into the sea; where in April and the beginning of May there come so many herring from the sea, which want to ascend that river, that it is quite surprising. This river the English have shut in with planks, and in the middle with a little door, which slides up and down, and at the sides with trelliswork, through which the water has its course; but which they can close with slides. At the mouth they have constructed it with planks like an eel pot with wings, where in the middle is also a sliding door, and with trelliswork at the sides, so that between the two there is a square pool, into which the fish aforesaid come swimming in shoals in order to get up above where they deposit their spawn, that at one tide there are ten thousand to twelve thousand fish in it, which they shut off at the rear in, the ebb, and close up the trellises above so that no more water comes in; then the water runs out through the lower trellises, and they draw out the fish with baskets, each according to the land he cultivates, and carry them to it, depositing in each hill three or four fishes, and in these they plant their maize, which grows as luxuriantly therein as though it were the best manure in the world; and if they do not lay these fish therein, the maize will not grow, such is the nature of the soil.

New Plymouth lies on the slope of a hill stretching east towards the seacoast, with a broad street about a cannon shot of eight hundred [feet] long, leading down the hill, with a [street] crossing in the middle, northwards towards the riverlet, and southwards to the land. The houses are constructed of hewn planks, with gardens also enclosed behind and at the sides with hewn planks, so that their houses and courtyard are arranged in very good order, with a stockade against a sudden attack; and at the ends of the streets there are three wooden gates. In the centre on the cross-street, stands the Govenor's house, before which four patereros [steenstucken] are mounted so as to flank along the streets.

Upon the hill they have a large square house, with a flat roof, made of thick sawn planks, stayed with oak beams, upon the top of which they have six cannons, which shoot iron balls of four and five pounds, and command the surrounding country. The lower part they use

SCALE MODEL OF THE PILGRIM VILLAGE—
Photograph courtesy of the Museum of Science, Boston, Massachusetts

for their church where they preach on Sundays and the usual holidays. They assemble by beat of a drum, each with his musket or firelock, in front of the captain's door; they have their cloaks on, and place themselves in order, three abreast, and are led by a sargeant without beat of drum. Behind comes the Govenor, in a long robe; beside him on the right hand comes the preacher, with his cloak on, and on the left the captain, with his side-arms and cloak on, and with a small cane in his hand; and so they march in good order, and each sets his arms down near him. Thus they are constantly on their guard night and day.

Their government is after the English form. The Governor has his council, which is chosen every year by the entire community by election or by prolongation of term. In the inheritance of children they place all the children in one degree, only the eldest son has an ac-knowledgement for his seniority of birth.

They have made stringent laws and ordinances upon the subject of fornication and adultery, which laws they maintain and enforce very strictly indeed, even among the tribes that live among them.

They speak very angrily, when they hear from the savages that we should live so barbarously in these respects, and without punishment.

Their farms are not so good as ours, because they are more stoney, and consequently, not so suitable for the plough. They apportion their land according as each has means to contribute to the eighteen thousand Guilders which they have promised to those who had sent them out; whereby they have their freedom without rendering an account to anyone; only, if the king should chose to send a Govenor-General, they should be obliged to ac-knowledge him as sovereign chief.

Their maize which they do not require for their own use is delivered over to the Govenor, at three guilders the bushel, who, in his turn, sends it in sloops to the north for the trade in skins among the savages. They reckon one bushel of maize against one pound of beaver's skin.

In the first place, a division is made according to what each has contributed and they are credited for the amount in the account of what each has to contribute yearly towards the reduction of his obligation. Then with the remainder they purchase what next they re-quire, and which the Govenor takes care to provide every year.

They have better means of living than ourselves, be-cause they have the fish so abundant before their doors. There are also many birds such as geese, herons, cranes, and other small legged birds, which are in great abun-dance there during the winter. The tribes in their neigh-borhood have all the same customs as already above described, only they are better conducted than ours, be-cause the English give them the example of better ordi-nances and a better life; and who, also, to a certain degree, give them laws, by means of the respect they from the very first have established amongst them.

THE ROLE OF THE CHURCH IN THE PILGRIM COMMUNITY

Since the Pilgrims had emigrated to America in order to obtain freedom of worship for themselves, it is not surprising that their church played such an important part in their community life, even assum-ing duties that today would be the function of the judicial system. Minor offenders were admonished by an elder of the church; those who had committed major offenses had to appear in the meetinghouse to confess their sin. The fort doubled as a jail but was seldom used for that purpose, an offender usually being fined and made to work for the good of the colony. The worst criminals were exposed to public shame in the stocks or, if incorrigible, whipped at the whipping post.

At first the fort served as the Pilgrims' meet-inghouse or church. Every Sunday the colonists spent much time there reading the word of God and testifying to His goodness, even when they had suf-fered sickness, death, and near-starvation. These trials they accepted as God's way of testing their faith, and they called on Him to give them strength to achieve their purpose, which was to establish His church in the land to which they had come.

A new building for the church was erected in 1648. This building doubled as a courthouse and a place for town meetings. A larger, handsomer church was built in 1683 on the site of the old one. It was at Plymouth that the Congregational Church originated; its members were not Separatists, but were in sympathy with the Puritans of the Massa-chusetts Bay Colony. The Congregational idea spread to the other colonies along the New England coast.

PILGRIM FAMILY LIFE

Just as the church was an important institution among the Pilgrims, so was the family. The feeling of family life was strong in most English people, and had been since feudal times, when to work the land demanded close cooperation between all members of a household. Craftsmen had their guilds, which represented a family on a professional scale, and in church the congregation was a family with ties to God. The pastor was a father figure, as

SUNDAY SERVICE IN THE PILGRIM VILLAGE

At first, the Pilgrims held their church services in the fort. Men were seated on one side, women and children on the other. The ladder leads to the gundeck.

was the lord of the manor, who depended on his family of peasants to sow and reap his crops. So it was at Plymouth, where each depended on the other for survival.

It should be understood that the Pilgrim household consisted of man and wife, plus children, not all necessarily their own, and male and female servants who were unmarried. The servants did not wait on the rest of the household, but worked along with the other members in performing tasks, both indoors and out. The man was head of the household, and worked at his craft or in the fields; his wife took care of the children, did the housework with the help of others, and prepared the meals. Males in the household worked for the master, the females helping the wife. Children other than babes did their share of the work, performing tasks suited to their strength and capabilities. Since medieval times this had been the form of the family and, as such, it continued until the Industrial Age, when the demand for labor in the factories caused changes.

Not all families lived in close harmony, particularly when a parent showed preference for a son or daughter over others in the household. The father was usually stern, and not to be challenged in any way, even by his wife, and children and servants alike had to do as they were told. For those who broke the rules punishment was apt to be harsh, and few liberties or pleasures were permitted. Colony life was hard, imposing on all discomforts and deprivations. There was little time for games for the young, even on Sundays, when nobody worked. Church services then filled their day. Youngsters were overseen by a deaconess who saw to it that none played or dozed off.

Despite the stern Pilgrim discipline, there must have been times when some children wandered out of sight of the village, as did young Billington, who in his wanderings discovered a "sea," which turned out to be a large pond. That chance wandering brought immortality to young Billington, after whom the pond is named, even to the "sea." There may have been those who snuck off with an Indian to learn how to set snares and traps, then later boast about their catch. There was no school in the village in its early days, so we do not know if parents who could read and write taught these skills to their children.

The regimentation of Pilgrim life may seem harsh to the modern reader, but there were reasons for it. The Pilgrims had a purpose to achieve which demanded the kind of disciplined life they imposed on members of their colony. There was no escape for any who did not obey these rules. Beyond the village palisade lay a country full of Indians and wild beasts; it was no place to face alone, and all knew this.

Chapter 5

How the Pilgrims Built Their Houses

ALTHOUGH much has been written on the buildings erected by the Pilgrims, nobody knows for certain just what the Pilgrim houses looked like. Bradford called the Pilgrims' houses small cottages, and other writers of the period say that some were "rude" and others "fair." A "rude" house may well have been one using the palisado technique of building; a "fair" house might have had a frame of heavy timbers, over which clapboards were placed; but this is mere conjecture.

The reason for building "rude" houses is made clear by Robert Cushman's statement to Bradford, who felt that the rather harsh terms made with the Adventurer's Company "will hinder the building of good and fair houses contrary to the advise of politics." Cushman, in answer, said, "So we would have it; our purpose is to build for the present such houses as, if need be, we may with little grief set fire and run away by the light." The Pilgrims' backers cared little what type of houses were built. Their

one interest was to receive payment in the shape of furs and other cargoes, to accumulate which would take time; so the less time spent in other pursuits, like housebuilding, the better. That these grasping merchants had no idea of the hardships the Pilgrims were enduring is borne out by their attitude, expressed in a letter to Bradford, in which they scolded the colonists for not sending back a cargo in the *Mayflower*.

Since it was decided that each family should build its own house, this factor alone would influence how each one looked. Francis Eaton, who was a carpenter, would build a better house than that of a man who had been a minor craftsman in Holland. Furthermore, a skilled workman would be able to erect his house at a faster pace than one with little or no experience. There must have been a certain amount of shared labor, and a swapping of skills; thatching is a skill only a farmer would have, and those skilled in the craft may have given their services in exchange for a supply of thatch, cut by others in the marshes nearby. A strong man may have assisted a weaker one in the puddling of clay for daubing over wattle set in walls and chimneys.

Archaeological evidence gives us a few clues, revealing the approximate size of a house, its hearthstone, and bits of window lead and glass (in later houses). One recent dig a few miles from Plymouth did reveal evidence of postholes, which suggest one kind of house construction, called palisado; town records reveal the fact that a number of houses were built this way, long after the Pilgrims landed.

In his description of the village houses de Rasieres raises more questions than he answers. The hewn planks to which he refers can be interpreted either as vertical boarding or horizontal clapboard, if the word "hewn" is interpreted freely. As mentioned previously, it is much easier to cleave a plank than to saw it from a balk of timber; with speed of the essence, the Pilgrims would surely have taken the easiest and quickest method of making the planks with which to sheathe their houses. They may have upgraded some of the "rude" houses at a later date by planking them but, for the most part, they would have filled between uprights with clay-daubed wattle. Their written records mention that heavy rains washed off some of their daub; this would be the weather side, proof of exterior daubing. If protected by an overhanging roof, clay daubing will stand up to most weather conditions other than driving rain. There are cottages in Devon, England, made of "cob," which is clay with a suitable binder. Snuggled into the landscape, and well protected with overhanging thatched roofs, they have outwitted the elements for over a century—proof that clay, if protected from moisture, is a sound building material.

CONTEMPORARY HOUSES OF ENGLISH PEASANTS

In trying to determine how the Pilgrims built their houses, English methods of construction are pertinent; for undoubtedly the houses which they built resembled those with which they were familiar in the England they left behind. The oak-framed house of the period is well known from the many examples still extant, but we should look

SECTION OF A WATTLE-AND-DAUB WALL

This wall remnant is preserved in the Town House museum, Poole, Dorset, England. Wattle fences are still common around Britain.

CARPENTERS ERECTING THE FRAME FOR A HOUSE

This old print shows a heavy timber being hoisted aloft with block and tackle. The timbers appear to be pegged together in the already erected framework.

more to houses of the peasants for a Plymouth prototype. The latter were still built in the medieval traditional style of one room. Such houses were built by driving corner posts into the ground and filling the spaces between them with smaller posts, also set in the ground. No sills were fitted, but the tops of all posts were mortised into the girts (beams supporting the rafters). Three principal rafters were fitted, one on each end and one in the middle, between which were set common rafters of smaller dimension. Tying the rafters together on each side were the purlins, which were set into the backs of the principal rafters to a depth which allowed the common rafters, when set upon them, to be flush with their face. Across the rafters were fitted long poles on which the thatch would lay. Built into the structure at one end was a framed wooden chimney, which was completed by filling the frame with woven twigs in the form of wattle, on both sides of which clay was daubed. This wattle and daub was used as a filling between the upright posts of the house, being cheaper than bricks and obtainable on

or nearby the house site. The lower end of the chimney flared into a hood over the hearth, which rested on a beam called the chimney breast. If the house had a loft, it was supported on rafters set into the "summer" beam (from the French *"sommier,"* a beast of burden or load carrier), which ran from the center of the chimney breast to the end girt. "Wind eyes" (windows) were few and made small, with an internal sliding wood shutter. The more affluent had windows made from horn, or paper painted with oil, over which were fitted twigs in a lozenge (diamond-shaped) pattern, to brace them against the wind. Later, in England this same pattern was repeated in leaded casements, available only to those who could pay the tax on glass windows. A door, made of a double thickness of wood, was fitted at the fireplace end. Its hinges were of wood or iron, and its wooden latch had a leather thong passing through a hole to the exterior for working the latch. This was pulled back inside at night to prevent unauthorized entry, in an age when thieves were plentiful. A strong wooden bar

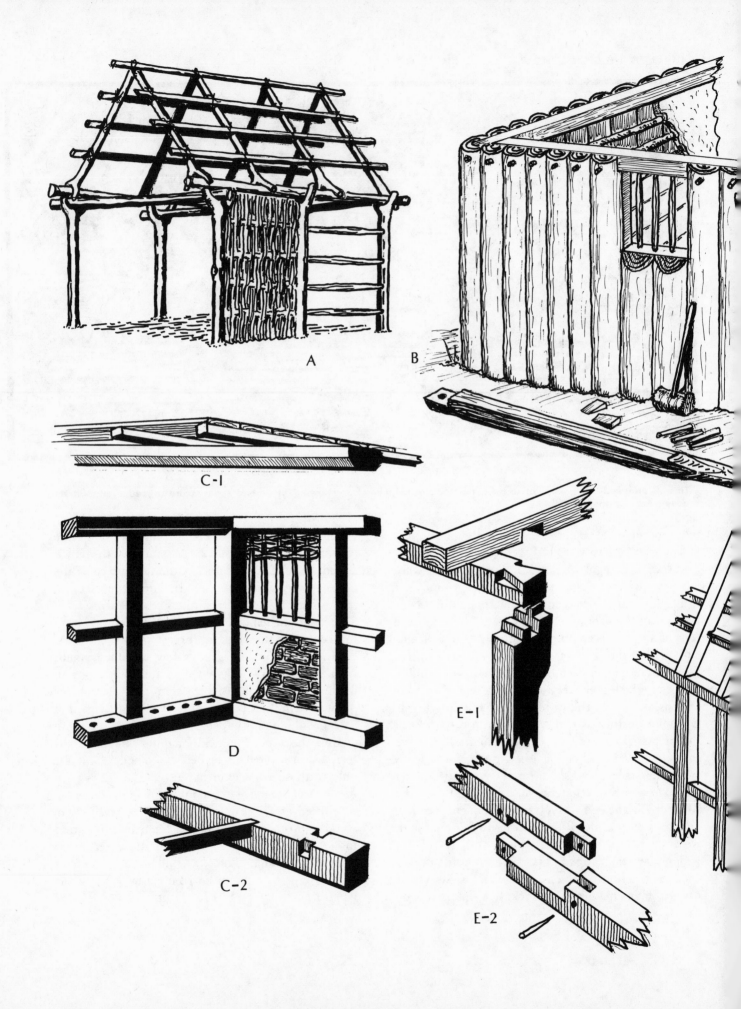

A

B

C-1

C-2

D

E-1

E-2

A. Anglo-Saxon house under construction. It is being made from tree trunks and branches, with wattle in-filling. Villages of such houses were surrounded by a palisade, much like that the Pilgrims erected around their village.

B. Saxon building under construction. This type of structure used split logs set into the ground and pegged to a frame for additional support. The palisado houses mentioned in New England town records of the seventeenth century may have been constructed in much the same way.

G. Tools used to construct the Saxon building. The maul and wedges were used to split logs. The maul also drove the wooden pegs which held the logs to the frame. The pick, crowbar, and spade were used to dig postholes. The tub holds clay mixed with chopped straw. This daubing was applied with a trowel, seen stuck in the clay. The bucket holds water for thinning the daub.

C-1. Attic floor beams laid on top of a summer beam.

C-2. Rafter mortised into a summer beam.

D. Early fifteenth-century house framing detail showing alternate methods of in-filling: (1) with woven wattle, over which lime mortar is plastered inside and out, and (2) bricks overlaid with lime mortar on both sides.

E-1. Sophisticated joint used in fifteenth-century house construction.

E-2. Seventeenth-century scarfing joint used to lengthen a timber.

F. Upper story of a medieval house frame, showing roof rafters and braced gable end.

G

was placed across the door inside, in case of attempted forcible entry. Often the house was incorporated with the byre in which oxen were kept. This served as a place for bodily functions, human wastes being added to those of the oxen. The loft above was a warm place to sleep in winter.

ARCHAEOLOGICAL AND HISTORICAL EVIDENCE

Recent evidence that the Pilgrims built their houses in similar fashion has been found in an excavated site near Plymouth, which indicates posthole construction; historical accounts can be cited as further evidence of the same method. Some evidence dates from a period later than 1620, but shows a persisting tradition. When, in 1629, Ralph Sprague and his companions arrived at Charlestown (now part of Boston), they found but one palisadoed and thatched house. This was a type of house that could be quickly erected by driving poles side by side to form the sides and ends of the structure. Evidence also exists concerning nine houses in Scituate (near Boston), "all which [were] small plaine pallizadoe Houses" (1627). A thief burglarized the house of a John Crocker "by putting aside some loose pallizadoes on ye Lords day."

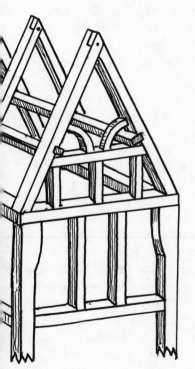

Marshall

Some experts, however, think this refers only to a fence around the house. Bradford makes mention of a hurricane which ripped off the roof of a house but left the corner posts still standing in the ground, thus giving credence to the theory that the Pilgrims' first houses were built in simple fashion, without ground sills. This is the opinion of the research staff at Plimoth Plantation in Plymouth, Massachusetts, where houses are now being built this way in the reconstruction of the Pilgrim village. These are small, one-room structures, with a partition at the end away from the fireplace, and a half-loft above. All posts are set in the ground, and the spaces between them filled with wattle and daub. Roofs are thatched with bulrush from adjacent marshes. Each house has a chimney of framed oak, daubed like the walls. A hood over the fireplace is similar to that of a medieval cottage, described above. The exterior of the houses are covered with hand-split clapboards. The interior floors are of packed earth. This type of house may be considered what Bradford called a "mean" house. We will next describe a "fair" house, built with more care in the English tradition.

To build a "fair" house would demand the skills of a trained carpenter, and the only one among the Pilgrims so qualified was Francis Eaton, as far as the records show. This type of house differed from the "mean" version by having its corner posts and uprights set into a sill laid on a foundation of stones. The sills were lap-jointed at each corner with a mortise made to take the tenon cut on the bottom end of the corner posts. The latter were thicker at their tops, to allow space to fit side and end girts (timbers on which the rafters rest). All structural timbers were first shaped and fitted on the ground, so that when time came to erect them, an assured fit was guaranteed. Corner posts were first set in place and temporarily braced, after which the upright posts were fitted. To lift the girts into place required the strength of several men, who had to make sure that the tops of the uprights fitted into the premade mortises. Once in place, all members were pegged together with wooden pins, which were previously dried over a fire to drive out moisture. When this moisture returned into the pegs from the atmosphere, they were very tight in place. The roof, similar to that described previously

for an English cottage, was next set in place, with the poles on which the thatch was tied. The hearth was of flat stones, with a backing of the same. After the house was erected the business of wattling and daubing commenced. There is an abundance of clay in today's Plymouth, so the Pilgrims would have had no trouble finding material with which to make the daub they plastered on the inside and outside of their wooden chimneys, and on the interior walls of their houses, as insulation against the cold of winter and heat of summer. It is doubtful if the Pilgrims burned sea shells to obtain lime for mortar, as this is a time-consuming process; thus we have to conclude that they used clay, which they puddled in a barrel and mixed with chopped reed to act as a binder. Wattle was put in place between the uprights, and daubed inside and out with clay. When dry, it was full of cracks, which were filled with more clay. The exterior of the house was then covered with overlapping clapboards. Lastly, door and windows were set in place, making the house ready for occupancy. It is entirely possible that some houses may have been sheathed with sawn boards, but not until a later date, since to saw boards took much longer than to split clapboards. Furthermore, sawn boards were inferior, in some ways, to clapboards, the cracks between them presenting a problem of caulking. Barns and animal sheds were more likely covered with sawn boards, little thought being given in those days to the comfort of animals, which were either beasts of burden or destined for the butcher.

Eighteen years after the Pilgrims came to Plymouth there is evidence that houses in New England were still being built much the same as in that colony. Deputy Governor Samuel Symonds of Ipswich wrote in a letter to John Winthrop: "Concerning the frame of the house . . . I am indifferent whether it be 30 foote longe; 16 or 18 foote broade . . . I would like wood chimneys at each end, the frames of the chimneyes to be stronger than ordinary, to beare good heavy load of clay for security against fire . . . ." Few bricks were then available; so there was no other alternative than to build as instructed. The Pilgrims suffered several fires due to this type of chimney construction, which, when clay fell away, allowed sparks to reach the tinder-dry wattle. A chimney afire meant al-

A THATCHED "FAIR" HOUSE

This reconstruction at Plimoth Plantation is a conjectural example of what one of the better Pilgrim houses may have looked like. Note the wood-framed wattle-and-daub chimney. The house in the background is in the process of being thatched.

most certain destruction of the thatched roof. By 1623 there were twenty houses in the Pilgrim village, four or five of which were said to be pleasant (fair). All had thatched roofs, but a succession of fires caused an act to be passed (in 1627) outlawing thatch in favor of "roofs of bord, or pale, or the like." "Roofs of bord" might have taken several forms, but most likely meant shakes (shingles), which are more easily and quickly made than boards. There are to be seen in old prints of the seventeenth century roofs made from planks. Gable ends are also shown planked. It may be that, with more time to spare, Pilgrim houses had more planking, but we do not know this for sure. Use of

planks required more nails, but these could now be produced in greater quantity with more smiths and metalworkers in the village.

TEMPORARY SHELTERS

Besides houses, a type of structure common in most of the early English colonies was the temporary shelter. Written records concerning the Massachusetts Bay Colony mention new arrivals who had to "burrow themselves in the earth for their first shelter under some hillside, casting the earth aloft upon timber." At Salem early arrivals are said to have built wigwams after the style of the

Indians. In England it was common practice for coppice workers and woodland craftsmen such as charcoal burners to build shelters from the wastes of the forest. Some of these were built like a tent, others had a slanting roof, open on one side, with a fire built along the front for heat and cooking.

The first Pilgrims to land were a working party which went ashore to cut timber for housebuilding, leaving the women, children, and those too sick to work aboard the ship. It was necessary to anchor the ship some distance from shore; this was inconvenient for the shore party, which had to row back and forth, sometimes against stiff winds and rough seas. Thus, there were times when they stayed ashore all night, living in hastily erected lean-tos made from tree branches covered with bark or turf. With a fire at the entrance, it was possible to keep fairly warm, and to cook hot food, a change from

weevily hardtack and "salt horse" (dried and salted beef). When weather kept them from the woods, they could fashion timbers under a shelter. Also, because the woods in which the Pilgrims worked to obtain building timbers were some distance from their village site, it was necessary to do all the processing of timbers at the place where the trees were felled. Here the Pilgrims would have erected temporary dwellings and a place to house their tools, which they were apt to leave on site.

WOODWORKING TOOLS OF THE PILGRIMS

The tools the Pilgrims brought with them were just as they came from the smithy where they were made, without wooden handles. In England it was the custom to work a coppice to glean wood for tool

TEMPORARY SHELTERS

Shown above is a portion of a print illustrating Nicuesa's expedition to Panama in 1595. It shows the erection of temporary shelters to house members of the expedition while they build a ship. It is quite probable that those Pilgrims working ashore at cutting timber for houses erected similar shelters in which to sleep when wind or tide prevented their return to the *Mayflower*.

handles and poles for use in training crops. A coppice is a woodland that has had its trees felled, but with the stumps left to sprout new growth. Ash and hickory were prized as the best woods to use for tool handles, since these trees grew straight and long, unhampered by the spreading branches of the trees, as in the original forest. The Pilgrims were familiar with this practice of working a coppice, and may have expected to find similar stands in the New World. Previous explorers of New England had reported the great stands of timber to be found there—oak, walnut, pine, beech, hazel, holly, asp (probably ash), and sassafras, the latter greatly prized as a medicine in Europe and used for a variety of ills.

A clue to the tools the Pilgrims used is found in this report from Plymouth written by Edward Winslow: "On Monday, the 25th day [December], we went on shore, some to fell timber, some to saw, some to rive, and some to carry, so no man rested all that day." Thus we know the Pilgrims had axes, saws, and splitting tools. "Some to fell timber" means they had axes, and these would include felling axes, side axes or broadaxes, and hatchets. The Pilgrims' axes would be similar to axes taken to Jamestown, the site of which has been excavated by archaeologists, bringing to light examples of axes and many other articles used in daily living in the seventeenth century. "Some to saw" indicates the Pilgrims made use of saws, which included a whipsaw (or frame saw), and a crosscut saw. The latter was not used to aid in tree felling, it came to be used for this purpose only in the nineteenth century. Rather, crosscut (or thwart) saw was used to cut trees to length. "Some to rive" indicates splitting tools: wedges and a tool called a frow (or froe), which was a thin wedge-shaped piece of iron with a socket at one end, into which a long handle was fitted. This was used to split billets of wood into clapboards. "Some to carry" means that timbers prepared in the woods, which were some distance from the Plymouth site, had to be carried by two or more men, if the piece was heavy; each man could carry a plank over his shoulder or on his head, as was a common practice at that time.

Another clue to tools of the Pilgrims is found in the following instruction which they issued to prospective colonists: "Let your meal be so hard trod in the cask that you shall need an adz or hatchet to work it out with." The adze and hatchet, however, were ordinarily used for other purposes. The adze was better suited for smoothing timbers to remove marks left by the side axe, surfacing floors, or shaping ship's timbers. The hatchet was a chopping tool, used mainly for providing firewood and roughly shaping timbers in carpentry work.

The felling axe excavated at Jamestown is eight inches in length and has a cutting edge three inches long. A blacksmith made it by folding a shaped length of iron around a mandrel, to form the socket for a handle. Before the folded iron was welded together, a piece of carbonized iron (crude steel) was inserted at the bottom edge. After welding, quenching, grinding, and tempering, the axe was helved, ready for use. The felling axe was sharpened on both sides. In use it was apt to bounce off a tree if not directed in a straight line. Unlike a modern felling axe, which is more square in shape, the seventeenth-century axe had no poll (weighted end) to better balance it in use. The side axe, or broadaxe, was so named for its shape and use, being much broader along the edge, and used to shape the sides of a timber when squaring up a round tree trunk. It was sharpened on one side only (like a chisel), so that the blade could lie flat against the wood being shaped. It came in two-handed and one-handed versions, and handles were offset to clear the wood being worked on. The hatchet was sharpened on both sides, since it was in essence a splitting tool. The frow was not made sharp like an axe, but was wedge-shaped to force apart the grain of the wood it was required to split. The adze, which is a type of axe with its blade crosswise to the handle, was sharpened on one edge only, the bottom being flat to get close to the wood.

In order to build a house, be it "mean" or "fair," the Pilgrims had to have a variety of other tools. Their later wills and inventories give clues as to what some of these were. It is quite likely that tools were supplied by their backers, and shared in common. Such tools would not appear in family inventories. To prepare a site for a house it was necessary to clear and level the ground on which it would stand. Hoes and spades would uproot any grass or weeds, and a rake would be used to comb the ground level.

GOING HOME LOADED

By "going home loaded" the Pilgrims meant returning home after a hard day in the woods, bringing back with them wood for their fires, material for weaving wattle, and timber for housebuilding.

HOW THE PILGRIMS BUILT THEIR HOUSES

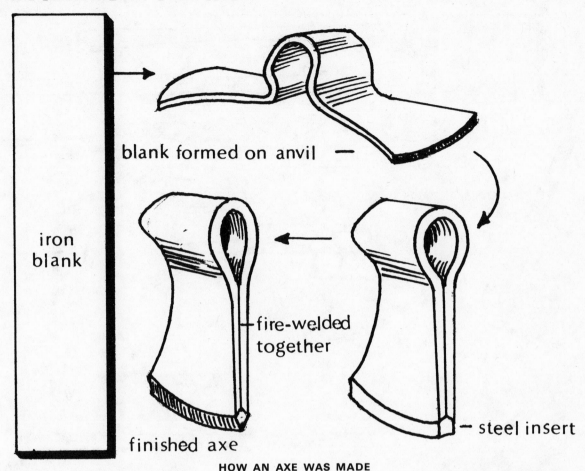

iron
blank

blank formed on anvil —

—fire-welded
together

finished axe

— steel insert

HOW AN AXE WAS MADE

Measuring and Marking Implements

Carpenters on the job would have rules for measuring—a ten-foot one for laying out and a two-foot version for smaller work. A carpenter would need a square, a bevel, a level, a pair of dividers for taking measurements off his rule, a scratch-awl for marking timbers, and a chalk line for marking planks to be rip-sawn. These tools have changed very little, the only differences being that modern tools are made of superior materials and slightly varied in style and shape.

Boring Tools

In addition to the tools mentioned, the carpenter carried in his toolbox, or basket, tools carpenters use to this day, including boring tools, hammer, mallet, chisels and gouges, pincers, crowbar, and shaping tools such as spokeshave and drawknife.

Since oak was a preferred building timber, it was used whenever available, as we know it was to the Pilgrims. This is a hard wood to bore, which, with the tools they had, took a long time. It was customary to make a starting hole for the boring auger by use of a gouge or, failing that, a red-hot iron the dimension of the auger. Smaller holes were made by the use of a "wimble," or brace, in which a boring bit was fastened. Nail holes were prestarted with a gimlet, a small screw-ended tool which was T-shaped when fitted with a handle. Nails were made of soft wrought iron, and would easily bend if the holes were not prebored.

HOW TIMBERS WERE SHAPED

To produce the variety of timbers necessary to build a house, much work had to be done. We will describe the steps taken in some detail.

TOOLS for working timber - 17th century-English.

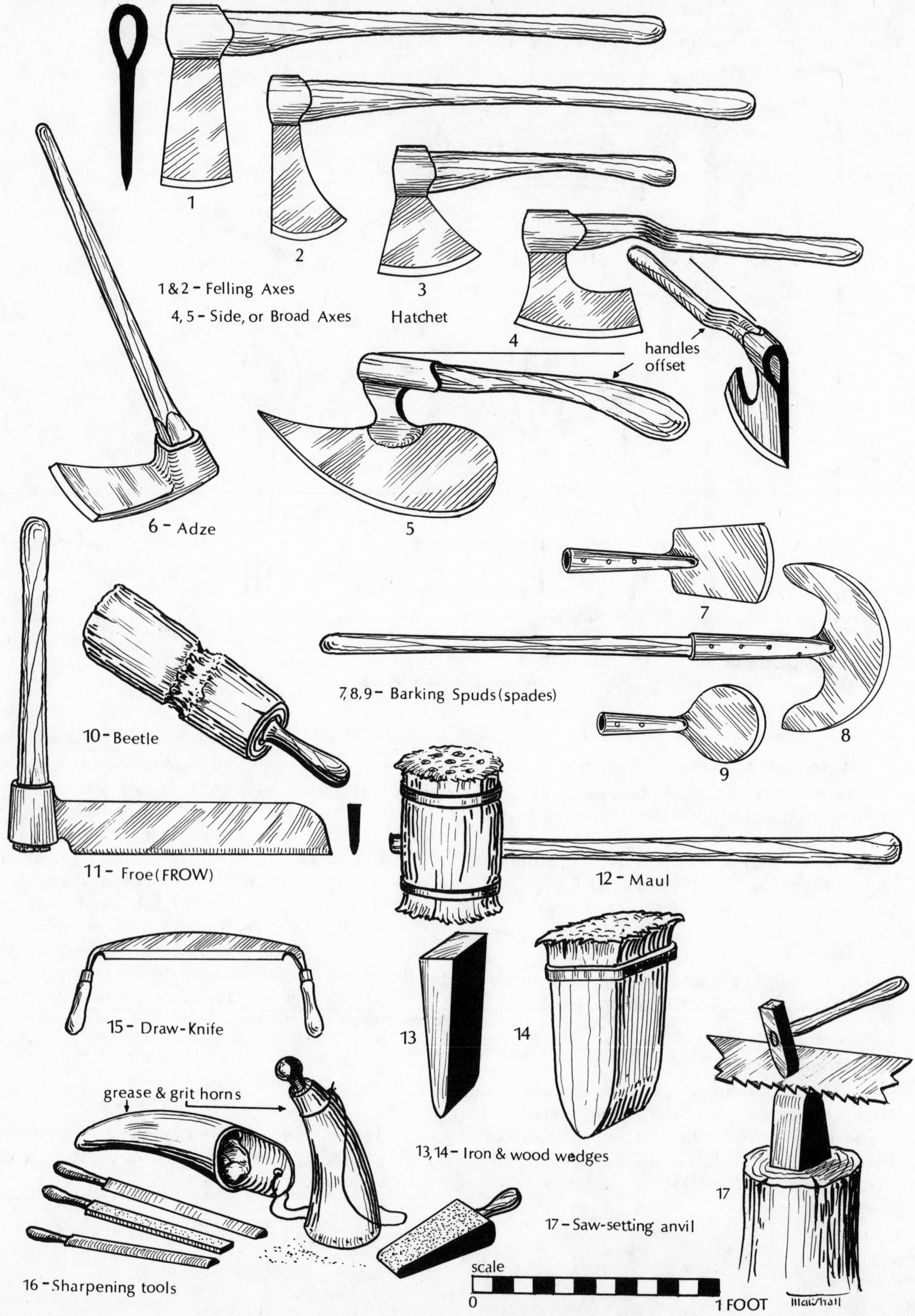

1
2
3
1&2 - Felling Axes
4, 5 - Side, or Broad Axes
Hatchet
4
handles offset
6 - Adze
5
7
7, 8, 9 - Barking Spuds (spades)
8
9
10 - Beetle
11 - Froe (FROW)
12 - Maul
15 - Draw-Knife
13
14
grease & grit horns
13, 14 - Iron & wood wedges
17
17 - Saw-setting anvil
16 - Sharpening tools
scale
0
1 FOOT
Marshall

17th century TOOLS for HOUSE BUILDING. LAYOUT & ERECTION

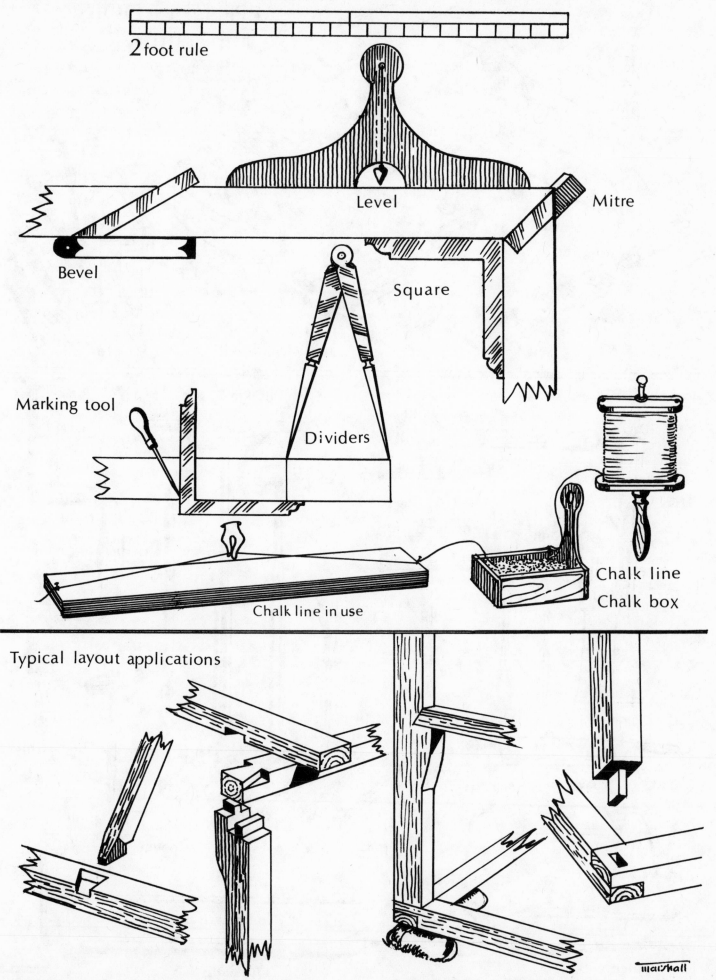

2 foot rule

Level

Mitre

Bevel

Square

Marking tool

Dividers

Chalk line

Chalk box

Chalk line in use

Typical layout applications

Marshall

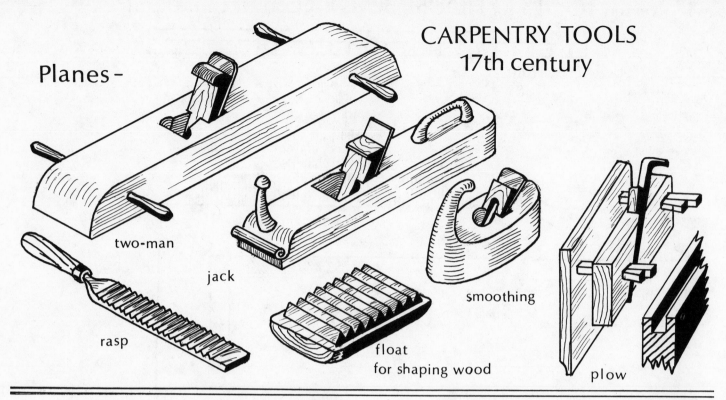

CARPENTRY TOOLS
17th century

Planes-

two-man

jack

rasp

float
for shaping wood

smoothing

plow

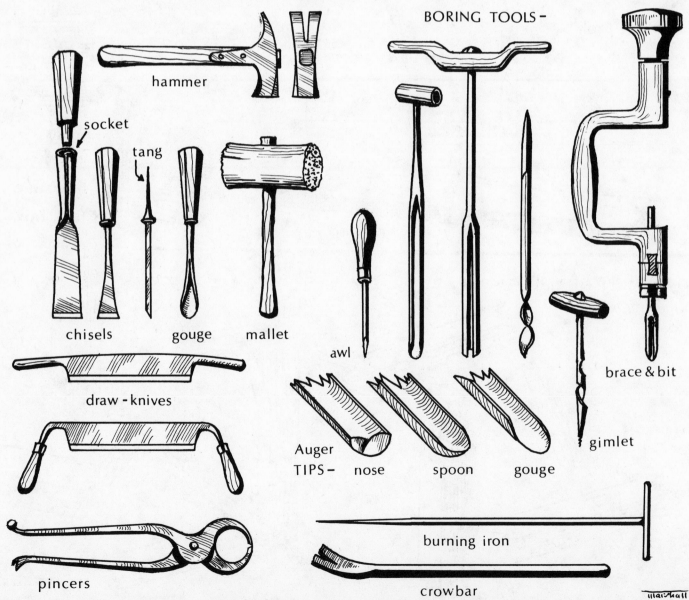

hammer

BORING TOOLS-

socket

tang

chisels

gouge

mallet

awl

Auger
TIPS-   nose   spoon   gouge

draw-knives

brace & bit

gimlet

pincers

burning iron

crowbar

The records tell us there were oaks abounding in the area, although not of great size. This was fortunate for those concerned with felling trees, since any of large dimensions would have required much chopping to achieve a fall. Frequent stops would have to be made to sharpen axes, dull ones being dangerous to use. Felling a tree in the seventeenth century was done differently from the method used today, in which chain saw has replaced the axe as a felling tool. The early colonists did not waste any of the tree, often making use of the main roots when a curved timber was needed. The first axe strokes were as close to the forest floor as possible, the axeman continuing more than halfway through the trunk before switching to the opposite side, which was then similarly chopped, the axeman ceasing when only a thin section remained between the two cuts. His last cuts were in the direction the tree would fall. The few final strokes presented some danger to the axeman, who had to be alert to the cracking sound made by the tree just before it fell. He moved rapidly away as the tree swayed and then crashed with a resounding thump between other trees in the forest.

Debarking Logs

As the axeman moved to another tree, men with side axes cut off the branches of the felled tree, setting them aside for further processing. When all branches were off, the tree was debarked with a barking spud (spade), the shape of which varied from round to crescent to rectangular, depending on the nature of the bark and how easily it came away from the wood. The bark was split along the length of the log, then peeled back in long lengths, the trunk being rolled to allow the underside bark to be removed. Bark in large pieces made good roofing for temporary shelters, and it was burned as fuel. Later, when the colonists processed leather, oak bark was used in the tanning process.

TREE-FELLING AND OTHER OPERATIONS

Squaring Logs

When the bark was peeled off, the side axemen went to work to make the round trunk square. To do this they made a series of slashes along the length of the log, then proceeded to remove slabs between them. After one side was done, it presented a square side from which the other sides could be marked, using a square. Work proceeded until all four sides were squared. Next came the adzeman, who stood astride on the top of the log, his legs wide apart. He swung his adze with one elbow against his side, thus controlling his swing. Working at an angle of forty-five degrees across the grain to avoid lifting it, he made his way down the log, erasing the marks left by the side axe.

Sawing Logs to Length

If the timber was to be a girt, it was then cut to length with the thwart, or crosscut, saw. These saws varied in tooth arrangement. Some cut one way only; others had the teeth cut alternate ways from the center, thus cutting on every stroke. Handles varied from upright to across the sawblade. Prints of the fifteenth century show saws of this type which had M-shaped teeth with gullets between them to allow sawdust to be brought out of the cut. This type reappeared in the nineteenth century, when the crosscut saw was used to fell trees.

Shaping Timbers Used for Corner Posts

A timber to be used as a corner post was shaped to roughly resemble a gunstock. This was to allow room for the placing of end and side girts when a house was framed. Heavy timbers such as these had to be dragged to the site with the aid of ropes and manpower. Lighter boards could be carried between two men, or on the head, as was the custom then.

Branches for Special Purposes

Tree branches were selected from the pile left by the axeman for special purposes. Slightly bent ones could be used as bracing timbers, smaller stuff being laid aside for the making of wattle fences or framing material on which clay was plastered to finish walls. Twigs made good fuel for fires; in fact, nothing from the tree was wasted, even the axe chips making good kindling.

Making Clapboards

Parts of the tree intended for making clapboards were cut to lengths of about four feet. These billets were then split by the use of iron wedges driven in along their length, forcing the grain apart. To release the wedges a blunter wooden wedge, called a "glut," was used. When driven into the split it usually completed the separation of the two halves. These were then split into quarters and handed over to the frowman. Placing his frow on the end grain, in a position to produce a thin wedge, he drove it down the grain with a "beetle" (club). When well into the billet, he pulled the handle towards him, tearing the grain further apart. If the billet was free of knots, it separated easily, each split-off piece being a rough clapboard. These were given to a man sitting at a shaving horse, a viselike device to hold the rough clapboards while he smoothed them with a drawknife. The smooth boards, about half an inch thick and tapering to zero at the lower edge, were used to sheathe the sides and ends of a house, and were placed overlapping from the bottom upwards, being nailed to the upright studs of the house frame.

Sawing Boards

If boards were to be produced, the procedure was more complicated. First, the squared timber had to be marked with a chalk line for the guidance of the sawyer. In use the line was rubbed with chalk, one end being held on the timber by one man and the other end at the farther edge of the plank by the chalker, who pulled it taut. Next, one man took the line between finger and thumb, raised it off the timber, and then let it snap back, where it left a chalk mark. These marks, made on top and ends, were set off in the widths desired. The timber was next raised by block and tackle hung from a tripod onto a trestle at one end. Then it was sawed with a frame saw, so called because the blade was mounted in a wooden frame, with means to strain the blade

LOG-SQUARING AND OTHER OPERATIONS

Upper left: Splitting a log by use of wedges. *Upper center:* Axeman slashing side of log to aid side axeman in foreground, who is squaring the timber for use in housebuilding. *At right:* Boy peeling bark from tree with a barking spud. Oak bark was used for tanning leather. Other barks were used for fuel.

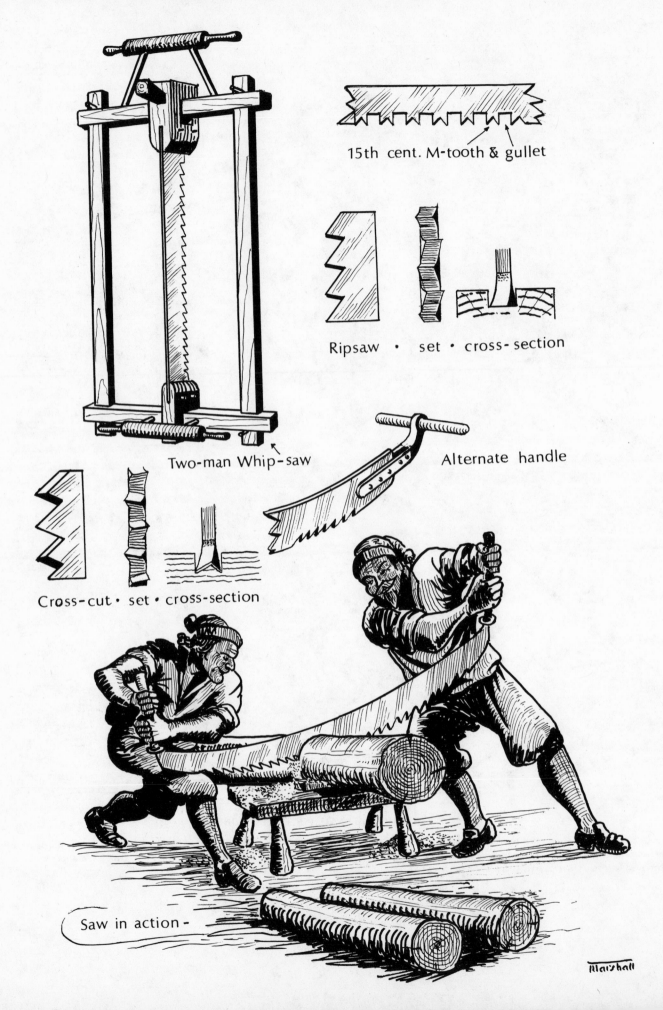

Two-man Saws - 17th century - English

15th cent. M-tooth & gullet

Ripsaw • set • cross-section

Two-man Whip-saw

Alternate handle

Cross-cut • set • cross-section

Saw in action -

Marshall

tight. The end where the saw would begin was supported by two stout oak props, notched to fit under the timber. Two sets of these props were used; their purpose was to make easier the passage of the frame holding the sawblade. Originally placed to the rear of the frame as sawing began, the props were removed after others were placed at the front of the frame, allowing free passage of the frame. Mounted on top of the timber was the boss sawyer, who grasped the "tiller," or top saw-handle. Below was the second sawyer, holding on to the "box," or lower handle. He did the actual sawing on the downstroke, the top man merely guiding the saw along the marked lines. The first cut was made down the center of the timber, to about halfway down its length. Alternate cuts were made to right and left of the first cut, until all lines had been sawn. The timber was then reversed and the process repeated. Sawing only to near center kept the timber intact as a stable platform for the top sawyer. When sawing was completed on both ends, the timber was lowered and split apart, the split-marks being smoothed away with an adze. Such sawing took a lot of time, and it is doubtful if the Pilgrims at first made use of this method to produce sheathing for their houses. There is evidence that the fort was sheathed in thick planks, and fences and outhouses may have been constructed with boards. Production of boards by this method was slow, made so by the need to re-sharpen the saw at frequent intervals, the constant necessity of removing the blade from one cut to start another, and the need to turn the log around at the halfway point. Bradford makes no mention of time taken in this operation, but from the nineteenth century there are records which show that it was possible for two men to saw four planks ten feet long, one foot wide, and two inches thick per hour. It is doubtful if the Pilgrims could have sawn at this rate, since in the later century saws were of steel that would keep an edge longer.

TOOL SHARPENERS

The means of keeping tools sharp were of the crudest in the seventeenth century. Grinding stones, made from sandstone and similar soft rock, were in use. Saw files were used to keep teeth sharp, but honing was done with a tool called a "skret," which varied in shape according to its use. It was made of wood upon which grease was smeared to hold grit sprinkled from a horn. An axe was first filed, then honed with the skret. Thomas Morton claims to have found grinding stones equal to those of Turkey. He was referring to very fine-grained sharpening stones which originated in that country. Craftsmen used them as honing stones.

Until the advent of good steel, all tools were made from wrought iron, which, when heated in a charcoal fire, took on the qualities of steel to some degree. Blacksmiths of the seventeenth century produced good tools using this method, but the problem of keeping a good edge on tools was left to the craftsmen who used them.

THATCHING ROOFS

Having covered the methods used to produce timbers for a house, and describing the tools used to erect them, we move up onto the roof to see how the thatcher did his job. The records tell us that some went to gather thatch, which presented no problem for the Pilgrims, there being marshes near their village site from which thatching material could be obtained. In East Anglia on the east coast of England, where some of the Pilgrims originated, there are extensive marshes which provided an assortment of materials useful to the thatcher. The best of these is the Phragmites reed, which is hollow but strong, with a waxy outer skin that sheds water. Growing alongside this reed is the common bulrush, with thick, cellular stems. This is used as capping material for thatched roofs. Certain broad-stemmed grasses are also sometimes used as capping material. Gathered in the spring, the reeds and grasses are spread out to dry, usually in the shade, then made up into bundles and tied. Transported to the building site, they are stored under shelter to keep them dry until ready to be applied.

Getting back to the Pilgrims, before the thatcher could go to work he had to build a scaffold on which to stand. He made several simple ladders for use in mounting the scaffold, and for use on the roof. The thatcher usually had a helper who worked inside the roof; others handed the bundles of thatch up to the scaffold, as needed. Working from right to left,

the thatcher laid bundles up the roof, angling them to present their stalk ends to the weather. After putting on the bottom layer, the thatch was again angled at the lefthand edge. As each bundle was laid it was tied onto the roof poles with tarred twine threaded through a long needle. Pushed through to the worker below, the twine was passed around the pole and back up to the thatcher, who then tied the bundle tightly. Some thatchers used staples of twisted hazel to hold down the thatch, pushing them over long rods placed across the bundles. These staples were also used to hold down the roof capping. Bundle after bundle of reed was tied to the roof poles to form a thickness of about two feet, the top bundles protruding above the ridge. Rolls of bulrush were then laid along the top of the roof, between the protruding reeds, which were then trimmed to the level of the top of the bundles. Next came the capping of rushes laid over the top of the bundles. This was held in place with long thin spars of hazel or willow, stapled in place. Criss-

THE SHAPING OF HOUSE TIMBERS FROM START TO FINISH

A. A timber being sawn into planks, after having been marked with a chalk line by the men behind the sawyers. The top sawyer guides the sawblade down the lines with the top saw handle, or tiller. The lower man, grasping the bottom saw handle, or box, pulls the saw downward to make the cut. Sawing is done down all the marked lines to the center; then the log is reversed and the procedure repeated. When the log is lowered from the trestle, the boards are split apart where they almost meet at the center, and the split-marks removed with an adze. *B.* Two men sawing a log to length with a thwart (crosscut) saw. *C.* Man splitting a log by driving a wedge into the grain with a maul. Nearby another man is using a side axe to square a log, as is the man shown at *D. E.* Man smoothing one side of a clapboard or shake (shingle). The workman is sitting on a shaving horse, a form of vise operated by foot pressure, which holds the wood being shaved against an inclined wedge. This smoothing process allowed the clapboards to fit tightly against each other. *F.* The rough boards were cleft from a log by beating a frow down into the grain and then levering off with the long handle. *G.* Finished timber being carried to the building site. *H.* A saw-setting anvil, inserted in the top of a log. On it the teeth of the saw were set at alternating angles, to prevent the saw from binding in the cut. A special hammer with a wedgelike head was used to set the teeth. *I.* A meal cooking in a pot suspended over a fire. The hard labor of shaping timbers built healthy appetites.

Hand-Saws of the 17th century - (shown in position used)

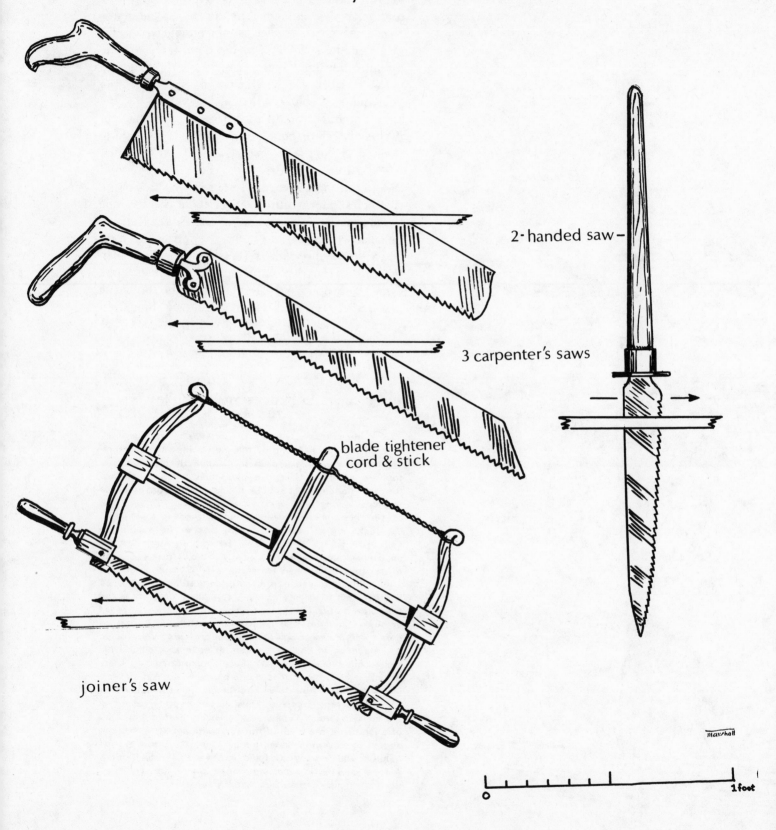

2-handed saw -

3 carpenter's saws

blade tightener
cord & stick

joiner's saw

0   1 foot

SHARPENING TOOLS · 17th cent.

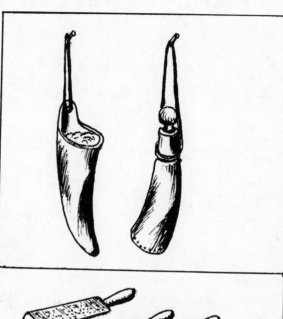

grease & grit horns
with sharpeners

grindstone

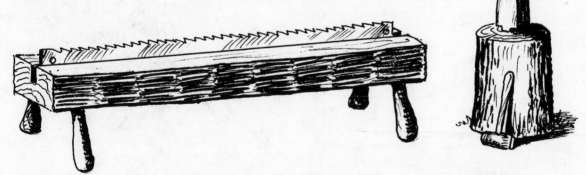

saw sharpening bench.   tooth setting anvil.

Marshall

Building materials from nature

MAXIMUM USE OF TREE

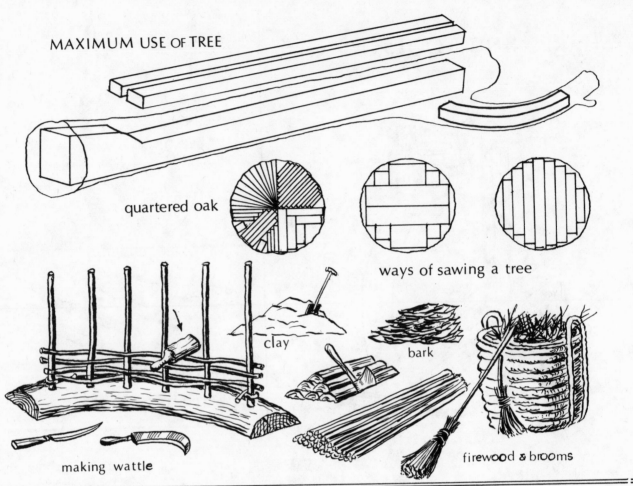

quartered oak

ways of sawing a tree

clay

bark

firewood & brooms

making wattle

THATCHING : Tools & method

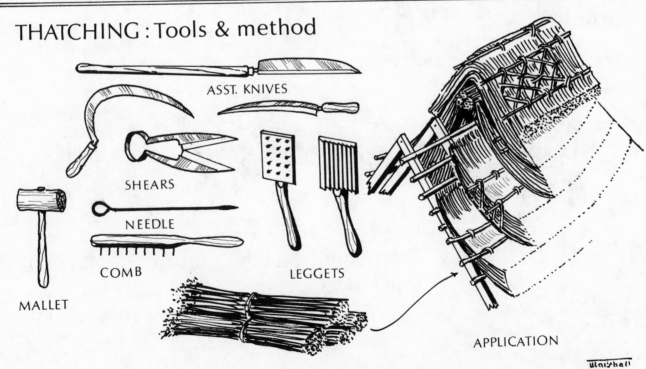

ASST. KNIVES

SHEARS

NEEDLE

COMB

LEGGETS

MALLET

APPLICATION

Marshall

BEATING UP THE THATCHING REED

The thatcher at Plimoth Plantation beats up thatching reed with a tool called a legget. Note its ridged surface. This beating exposes the ends of the reed to the weather, making a tight roof. Such a roof will last over fifty years.—*Photograph by Thomas J. Croke*

crossed sticks were set between these spars, and stapled in place. The bottom edge of the capping was cut with a long, sharp knife. Around the chimney wet clay was placed to keep out rainwater.

Thatching Tools

All the work of thatching was done with very simple, but special tools. To beat the rush up so that only its ends were exposed to the weather, a tool called a legget was used; one type was ridged, and had an offset handle. To both comb and beat up the reed, another type of legget had large-headed nails set into its surface. Other tools used by the thatcher were a long knife for trimming, a short one for cutting the twine, a pair of trimming shears, a wooden mallet, and a long iron needle. Before a

bundle of reed was put in place the thatcher dropped it at an angle on his "butting board," a flat board about two feet square. With one helper aloft and one below, the thatcher could lay bundles and tie them in place in short order. We know from records kept by the Pilgrims that it took them four days to thatch half of their common house. This gives us an estimate of the time it took to thatch a building measuring twenty feet square. Completing a roof such as that on a Pilgrim cottage took about two weeks, depending on the weather.

With a roof overhead a family could move in and start to live the hard life of colonists, working from sunrise to sunset, snatching a meal when possible, then curling up on a bedroll for an uneasy sleep. Next we shall follow these colonists through their daily tasks of meal preparation and housekeeping.

Chapter 6

Meal Preparation and Housekeeping

It is not surprising, in view of the months of near-starvation endured by the Pilgrims after they landed at Plymouth, that securing food was one of their most time-consuming tasks. During the starving times when large game was scarce the Pilgrims were forced to eat anything that could furnish a little meat. With traps and snares, which they were taught how to make by the Indians (see Chapter 8), they caught squirrels, rabbits, and even rodents. Morton, who lived with the Indians when seeking furs, tells of eating blackbirds, which he said resembled veal. Morton, a fastidious English gentleman of sorts, never seemed to mind what he ate, whether it were raccoon, bear, or beaver, the "stones" of which he particularly relished. The turkey, long a symbol of Thanksgiving, was not frequent food on Pilgrim tables, if we take the word of archaeologists, who found few turkey bones in Pilgrim sites. In any case, the wild turkey was a skinny bird compared to the fattened-up variety sold today. The

Pilgrims shot and ate swans, ducks, geese, and even small shore birds, some of which taste pretty fishy. The better shots must have spent many hours afoot or concealed in the marsh to obtain food. There were fish to be caught and a chance deer to be stalked and killed. Venison was particularly relished, inasmuch as in England it was available only to those owning large shooting preserves. Moreover, one deer made food for several families, whereas it took several game birds to fill a pot. Hunting was usually done in pairs, so that, should a deer be shot, it could be carried on a pole between the hunters. One could load a musket while the other fired, thus saving time between shots. The shore was visited as a last resort; there a lobster or two could be fished out from under the rocks, or a mess of mussels gathered.

There is written proof that meals prepared in Pilgrim households were good. John Pory, who visited the colony in its early years, wrote: "The wholesomeness of the place, and its healthfulness is accompanied by so much plenty of fish and fowl everie day in the year, that I know of no place that can match it." He was fortunate enough to arrive when the pots were full, and could not say enough for the lobsters served him, although he did regret the absence of oysters at Plymouth. Perhaps he did not care for mussels, which were plentiful. Thomas Morton, who also visited Plymouth, highly praised the fish he was served there. Although the Pilgrims had become sick from eating clams when they were anchored off Cape Cod, they use them for making chowder and fish cakes. Eels, of which they had an abundance, they ate with relish. The records tell of taking a hogshead of eels in one night. This was a delicacy that the Leyden Pilgrims would have enjoyed in Holland, but never in such quantity. Eels could be fried, boiled, or pickled, and tasted good no matter how prepared.

HOW THE PILGRIMS PRESERVED THEIR FOOD

Even in good times the Pilgrims did not neglect to provide for the long winter when fresh food was scarce. Bradford mentioned the need for a salt pan in the colony. A salt pan consisted of a low-lying area near the shore which could be flooded at high

EEL TRAPS

The Pilgrims used traps like these for catching eels. Inside the wide mouth of each trap is a cone with a small opening in its end. Eels can swim into, but not out of, these traps. Such traps, made from willow or hazel osiers, have changed in shape very little over the centuries.—*Photograph by Thomas J. Croke*

Salting down meat and fish

from an old print

from an old print
of 1618

tide, then closed off. The sun would evaporate the seawater, leaving behind a salt crust which could be gathered and stored in barrels. However, despite the need the colonists seem never to have constructed such a pan. To salt down meat or fish took a lot of salt, which could be obtained only by boiling water from the sea until it evaporated, a long process if any amount of salt was to be obtained.

Smoking Fish

The Indians cured their fish by placing them on a rack set over a smoky fire, or in the hot summer sun. No doubt the Pilgrims did the same, as they would be familiar with the process in their native land whereby meat was placed on hooks in the chimney, where the smoke and heat dried it. Before drying, the fish were slit down one side and laid flat, the bones being removed at this time. These fish, when left drying in the sun, had to be protected from seagulls, which were not averse to a free meal, easily obtained in one swoop. Children were posted to shoo them away, as they were to guard the ears of corn in the fields at their time of ripening.

The Pilgrims, when smoking their cod, were unaware of the nutritional value of the oil from its liver. If they extracted it, they would have used it as fuel for their crusie lamps.

MEAT AND DAIRY PRODUCTS

Until meat became more plentiful, it was a minor part of the average diet, an eater having to fill his stomach with corn gruel or corn bread. When livestock was introduced, the colonists must have relished a piece of beef, mutton, pork, or even goat flesh, after years of salted meat and fish. Chickens provided them with eggs and an additional source of meat. When an animal was slaughtered for meat, it was not cut selectively as it is today; meat was meat, and likely tough, even in the tenderloin. Before being served, meat was treated in several ways to make it more palatable. It was beaten to make it more tender, or cut up small to put into pies. Herbs were crushed and rubbed on the meat or boiled in the pot to add flavor.

After the arrival of cattle in the colony in 1624 there was more work for the women to do. They milked the cows and skimmed the milk of its cream to make butter and cheese. These dairy products were a welcome addition to the daily diet, giving extra calories, which were needed for the hard work performed by the men. A worker in the forest, housebuilder, or field hand needed around 5,000 calories per day, and so ate accordingly.

EDIBLE WILD PLANTS

Although many of the Pilgrims with a rural background would know how to find natural fruits and nuts, it was the Indians who showed them how to find tubers in the earth that made good eating (see chapter 8). Many wild plants were good to eat as vegetables, and these were eagerly sought in season. Some may have found a place in Pilgrim gardens, to save a long hike into the countryside to obtain them.

FOOD FROM PILGRIM GARDENS

The Pilgrims, typically English, loved their gardens, which were highly praised by Josslyn when he visited the colony. He was particularly taken with the abundance of herbs grown; the pumpkins when cooked he likened to stewed apples. Lacking wheat and barley, to which they were accustomed at home, the colonists had to learn to like corn, which was a staple food of the Indians.

DEVICES FOR GRINDING GRAIN

We know that the Pilgrims brought over English grain, because Bradford speaks of it not thriving; so they must have brought over a device to grind grain into flour. The common household instrument for

SALTING DOWN MEAT AND FISH

Top: An illustration of preserving meat, taken from a sixteenth-century print. Preserving meat by packing it in salt was a team effort. The butcher chopped the cuts into convenient size and handed them to the man at the salt tub. In the tub the butcher's helper alternated layers of meat and salt. The cask was then headed and put in a cool place until needed, usually in winter when fresh meat was scarce. *Bottom:* An illustration of preserving fish, taken from a print of 1618. It shows a woman gutting a fish, together with a helper. Gutted and laid flat, the fish were then dried and smoked over a fire, or packed whole in lots of salt, as was done by European fishermen who fished off Maine and Newfoundland. Doing this work on the beach saved effort, and seagulls and fish acted as scavengers when the refuse was disposed of in the sea.

Harvesting Tools - 17th century

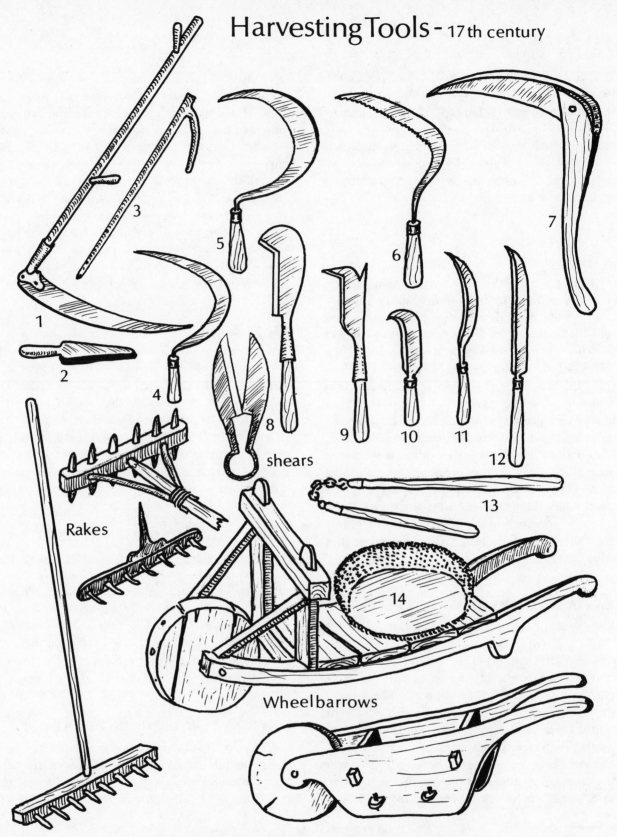

3

5

7

1

2

4

6

8 shears

9 **10** **11**

12

13

Rakes

14

Wheelbarrows

HARVESTING TOOLS OF THE SEVENTEENTH CENTURY

1. Scythe. In use this type of scythe was not swung in an arc, as were later models with a curved handle, but was pulled towards the reaper with a chopping motion. Such scythes appear in prints by Brueghel. *2.* Skret, a sharpening device for the scythe. This was often little more than a wooden shape on which grit and grease were smeared to act as an abrasive. Later on, so-called turkey stones were used to sharpen tools. *3.* Reaping hook. This was used to pull stalks of grain towards the reaper using a sickle to cut them. *4, 5, 6,* and *7.* Sickles. The shapes and cutting edges vary, according to the crops they were used to cut. No. *7* is a corn knife. *8* and *9.* Billhooks. Used to cut brush, these implements varied according to region, but all are heavy and curved in some way. *10.* Pruning knife. *11* and *12.* Slashing knives for cutting brush or harvesting reeds for thatching. During the latter process they were used to trim the reeds when topping out the roof. *13.* Flail. This was used to beat the grain from its stems. *14.* Winnowing basket. Flailed grain was tossed in this basket in a windy place to get rid of chaff.

Wheelbarrows. The open type was used to cart wood or sacks; the bottom type for carting manure or soil.

Rakes. These were originally made of wood, but an early iron type is also shown. The double-tined type appears in a Brueghel print.

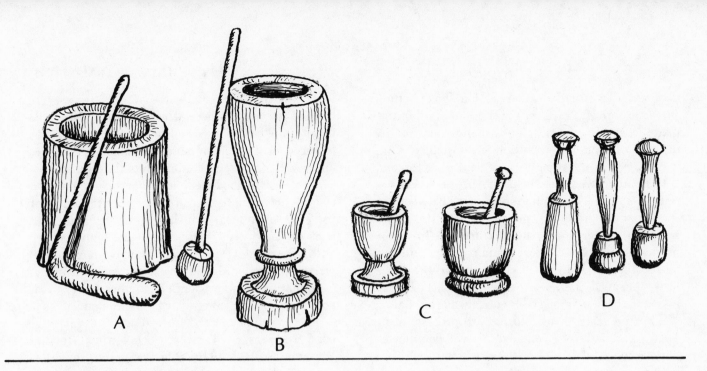

not to scale

Marshall

HOUSEHOLD AIDS

A. Pounding mortar made from a hollowed-out log. *B.* Shaped wooden mortar for pounding corn and other grains. *C.* Small wooden mortars and pestles for crushing herbs and spices. *D.* A variety of wooden pestles. *E.* Sixteenth-century bell-metal mortar and pestle. *F.* Seventeenth-century bell-metal mortar and pestle. *G.* Coopered butter churn with handle of paddle protruding. *H.* Two types of paddle used in a churn.

this was the quern, consisting of a fixed bottom stone on top of which was a stone of similar size made to revolve by means of a handle set into its top. Also in the top was a hole, down which grain was poured as the stone was rotated. Both top and bottom stone were channeled, as in the larger variety in a mill. The grain found its way between the channels and out at the sides. The way the stones were cut determined the texture of the flour produced. Of course, before grinding, the grain was flailed (beaten with a stick) to remove the outer husk. Scooped into a winnowing basket, it was tossed in the air, the wind blowing away the chaff.

The Indian corn was too hard to process in the quern, and had to be pounded in a wooden mortar with a pestle, after which it was ground finer in a bronze mortar with a metal pestle. Even with all this pounding it was impossible to make a fine flour, but the meal served to make gruel and journey cakes (johnny cakes). A pudding made from this grain was a favorite with most. In time the colonists got their native grains to grow, and could use less corn, which they still continued to grow to sell to other colonies, and to the Indians in Maine, where land to grow corn was not available.

HERBS AND OTHER SEASONINGS

Condiments such as pepper and seasonings from the Orient had no place in Pilgrim cooking, their function being performed by herbs grown in the colonists' gardens. Some of the herbs introduced by the Pilgrims to America were basil, balm, chives, fennel, lovage, mint, parsley, rosemary, sage, and thyme. Basil served many uses, being used in soups, stews, and salads, and for flavoring vinegar. It was also much valued as a fly repellent. Rosemary, which was a moth repellent, and other sweet-scented herbs were put among clothes in chests. Thyme, rosemary, and lemon balm were planted to attract bees, which furnished the only sweetening the Pilgrims had.

Few needed salt when a lot of their food was preserved in it. Since it was a long process to boil salt from seawater, it was used sparingly.

Recipes were those of the cook of the day. Despite the fact that cookbooks had been around since the fourteenth century, it is doubtful if there were any at Plymouth, since most of these were printed for use by those who cooked to satisfy the jaded appetites of the well-to-do. Such cookbooks featured exotic, highly spiced dishes; rich gravies and sauces were served on much of the food and accounted for a good deal of dyspepsia among the rich. Some of these sauce recipes were intended for use with salted meat, which even the rich had to fall back on in winter. Such sauces were highly spiced with ginger, cloves, cardamom, or cinnamon, and were often colored and flavored with saffron. A combination of nuts pounded together with raisins and mixed with vinegar was recommended as a sauce for salted meat. Mustard and vinegar were used freely as condiments. Such fancy flavorings were not available to the Pilgrims; so just how they coped with salted meat we do not know.

BEER AND OTHER BEVERAGES

Naturally, with salted meat and fish forming such an important part of the Pilgrim diet, beverages were important to the colonists. Bradford had boasted of the fine water they drank at Plymouth, which was pure in his day. Few drank water in Europe unless sure of its origin, preferring beer as a beverage. The Pilgrims loved their beer. At first the Pilgrim women made it from roasted sprouting corn. They made this into a mash for fermenting with wild yeasts. The beer brewed was flavored with herbs, hops not being then available. Every family brewed beer according to its own formula. The finished product was low in alcoholic content and had no resemblance to the modern brew, but it suited the colonists, who were used to drinking it in preference to water. Later, with grain like barley to work with, the Pilgrims could brew a better beer.

Brandy and gin were used mostly for medical purposes, and could not have been in large supply in the colony. While no tea or coffee were available to the colonists, it was common to drink herbal infusions to quench thirst or for reasons of health.

THE HEARTH

There was little difference in food at each meal, there then being no breakfast foods, lunch snacks,

MAKING BEER

The woman is stirring the mash while the man in the rear scoops grain out of a sack.

or packaged dinners. All simply ate what was available. The first meal of the day was always ample (in good times), and might consist of corn gruel, griddle cakes, and some meat, washed down with beer. Men going far afield to work might take food with them to save a trip back to the house, but they would come home prepared to eat a large evening meal. All this meal preparing took the time and efforts of several of the female members of the family. Naturally, much of this labor centered around the fireplace.

The Fire

The fire was kept alight day and night, because of the difficulty of starting a new blaze with flint and steel. From time to time a fire would die down and need to be rekindled; this was done with a pair of bellows, which quickly fed more oxygen to the flame. The fire consisted of a backlog from which embers could be chipped with a fire fork for the several fires needed on the hearth. Over the backlog hung a large kettle, supported on a trammel, an adjustable hook suspended from a wooden lug-pole set into the chimney. In this at any one time might be water for the family wash, a stew, or even a complete meal, depending on the need. Because of an early lack of iron, the lug-poles were made of wood, which in time dried out and broke, often when a pot was full. It is to be hoped that Doctor Fuller had in his kit salves for scalds and burns, to use when such accidents occurred.

Cooking Utensils

Visitors to antique houses often come away with the impression that there was little room around the fireplace for other than the vast assortment of

SEVENTEENTH-CENTURY FIREPLACE EQUIPMENT

Shown in the fireplace are the means for hanging pots over the fire. From a lug-pole in the chimney hung adjustable trammels. The chain type came first; then ratchet and alternate-hole types. The crane, although widely used in England in the seventeenth century, appeared later in America. Fire dogs, andirons, and trivets were common to most hearths.

The cooking utensils and tools shown to the right of the fireplace include a meat fork, spoon, slice (spatula), skimmer, and ladle. On the shelf are a clay jar and pipkin, the latter being used over live coals like a saucepan. On the floor rests a frying pan. Some frying pans, called "spiders," had legs. Also shown are a pan for catching the drippings from cooking meat and a brass milk jug. On the wall hangs a pair of bellows, used to revive a dying fire.

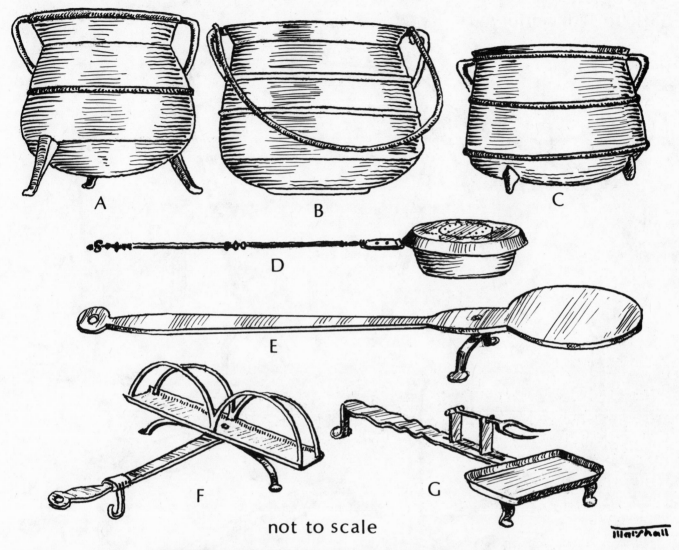

not to scale

SEVENTEENTH-CENTURY COOKING AND FIREPLACE UTENSILS

A. Kettle found at Jamestown, Virginia. *B.* Kettle from the seventeenth-century house in Hereford, England. *C.* Kettle reputed to have belonged to Myles Standish. It is now in Pilgrim Hall, Plymouth, Massachusetts. *D.* Bedwarmer with hinged brass lid and wrought iron handle. In the eighteenth century wooden handles became common. *E.* Down-hearth salamander (literally, a dweller among fire). This was used like a girdle (griddle) to cook flat cakes and bread. *F.* Fish roaster, pivoted to turn fish so as to cook both sides. *G.* Meat roaster with adjustable fork and drip-pan.

cooking gear. This was not the case in Pilgrim households, if we can believe their inventories of household equipment. They had to manage with a few pots and saucepans. This is why they often cooked a whole meal in the big pot on the back of the fire. By suspending food in net bags, along with the meat, the Pilgrims cooked all together, caution being taken to put the vegetables in when the meat was about cooked. Gravies and the like were made over a small ember fire at one side of the hearth.

Smaller fires were set under saucepans with built-in legs; legless pans were set on iron stands called trivets. A large covered kettle, called a dutch oven, was used for baking bread and stewing meats. It was buried in hot ashes, and its cover heaped with glowing embers. Cakes made from cornmeal were baked on a "girdle" (griddle), and fish was cooked in a long-handled skillet.

Logs were set on fire dogs, which raised them up to allow a better draft. These fire dogs were fitted

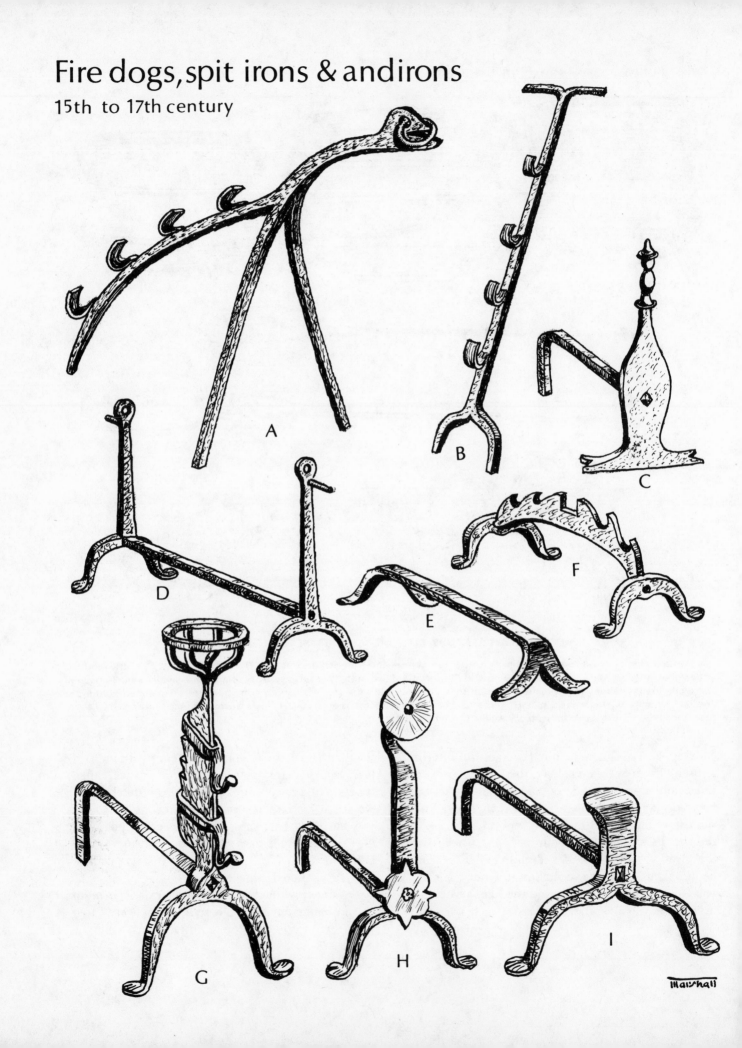

Fire dogs, spit irons & andirons
15th to 17th century

A

B

C

D

E

F

G

H

I

Marshall

on their front with a series of hooks on which a spit was placed when roasting meat. In use a piece of meat or a bird was slid onto the spit, at the center of which were prongs to prevent the meat from twisting. The cook turned the spit from time to time to brown the meat on all sides. Under the spit was set a drip-pan, a long iron container to catch the fat, which was saved for use in soapmaking. For roasting meat, logs were sometimes slanted on cob irons to reflect the heat upwards. When fowl was on the small side, several birds might be slid onto the spit but, more often, they were baked in a pie or in the dutch oven, cooking in their own juices. Meat intended for future use was hung in the chimney for smoking.

Fire-tending Implements

The art of using the burning logs in the fireplace was one of utilizing all sides when preparing a meal, or placing, by use of fire tongs, each log where it would best serve the cook. To distribute embers a fire shovel was used, as it was for the removal of ashes which accumulated on the hearth. These were saved to make lye, used in soapmaking. To keep the fires replenished, wood taken from a larger supply outdoors was piled at the side of the hearth. Hardwoods were preferred for cooking, being longer-burning and often more aromatic than softer woods. The hardwood ashes were also preferred for lye-making, producing a stronger product than soft woods.

COOK'S TOOLS

The cook had need for many small tools, such as a ladle, skimmer, and strainer. These hung on hooks within her reach. In preparing a meal the housewife would set up a table on trestles as a place for her mixing bowls, colander, meat-cutting board, and mortar, and pestle, with which herbs were ground or meal made finer. The table would be left in place for the evening meal, covered with a cloth, and supplied with large napkins of linen.

MEALTIME ETIQUETTE

In the absence of chairs, most meals were eaten standing, each diner reaching into the common bowl or platter with fingers, which, as the saying goes, were made before forks. Eating with the fingers is messy, and napkins were a necessity. Even the nobility of that day ate this way, and cleaned up in similar fashion, sometimes being served with bowls of rosewater in which to dip their smelly fingers before wiping them. Forks were lacking at Plymouth, as they were with a few exceptions at Jamestown. What few were there belonged to the gentlemen, who in the homeland had lived with some elegance. Knives and pewter spoons were the dining tools in both colonies.

TABLEWARE

The poverty of the Pilgrims may be deduced from the lack of ceramic ware of any quality. They did have cooking ware and a few pieces of stoneware of European origin (possibly Dutch). This is in contrast to Jamestown, where there was an abundance of ceramics found in dug sites. The Plymouth colonists must have had much woodenware, which they could make themselves. Early plates were small and square, with a circular area scooped out to hold the food. Since the latter was served up in a common bowl the plate did not need to be large, serving more as a drip-catcher than as a place to stack food. There may have been some pewterware in the colony, particularly flagons for beer, and

FIRE DOGS, SPIT IRONS, AND ANDIRONS OF THE FIFTEENTH TO SEVENTEENTH CENTURY

A. True fire dog (also a spit iron). The fire dog resembled a dog or animal; hence the name. *B.* Spit iron (one of a pair). This was made to lean against the back of the fireplace. Iron spits were placed upon its hooks for roasting game or birds. *C.* Sixteenth-century andiron, made of wrought iron, with a brass finial. *D.* Another type of fire dog, dating from the time when fires were built in the center of the great hall of a castle. Logs were leaned against the crossbar alternately on each side. *E* and *F.* Cob irons. *E* was used when logs needed to be inclined to make a fire for roasting meat on a spit. *F* is also a form of spit iron (used as a pair). *G.* Andiron with brazier top and adjustable spit hooks. The brazier could hold live coals for heating a small saucepan or a pine knot to give light near the fireplace. *H.* Seventeenth-century andiron with brass decorations. *I.* Seventeenth-century andiron common to most households.

CERAMICS OF THE SIXTEENTH AND SEVENTEENTH CENTURIES

Left: Jug of Rhenish ware, imported into England. *Top center:* The development of the clay smoking pipe. It was made small when tobacco was scarce and expensive; larger as tobacco was produced in quantity in the Virginia plantations. *Top right:* Pipkin, a cooking pot of cream paste with a yellow glaze. It was in use from medieval times until it was replaced by iron and brass pots. *Bottom center:* Feather-combed dish and marbled dish, both of the seventeenth century. *Bottom right:* Bellarmine bottle, circa 1600. It was supposedly named after Cardinal Bellarmine, a persecutor of Protestants during the Counter-Reformation. Actually, these bottles were made to hold wine before Bellarmine's time. The mask was said to be that of the pagan Gallic god Esus, probably a variant of Zeus. It was made of stoneware and overlaid with a gray or brown salt glaze, first in the Rhineland and later at Fulham, England, in the late seventeenth century.

bowls for the cook's use. Pewter spoons were quite common, and could be home cast if molds were available. Casting was common in the making of balls for muskets, and Standish may have put men to work doing this as part of their military training. Glass was scarce, bottles being the most common, and these were usually those that held liquor (brandy and gin). Besides pewter, drinking vessels were made from horn, ceramic, or wood (flagons "coopered-up" like barrels). During a meal it was common practice to pass around a flagon from mouth to mouth, and, to make this easier some drinking cups had two or more handles. Salt was placed in a small pewter or ceramic container near the head of the table. Later salt cellars had three

prongs rising from their sides, over which a napkin was placed to keep out moisture.

CLEANING AND SOAPMAKING

Utensils were cleaned after each meal with ashes to absorb grease, and rinsed in water. Pewter took on a pleasant luster when so cleaned.

Cooking, cleaning, and the family wash demanded a lot of water. This had to be hauled in buckets from a spring in the village, a task assigned to children, aided by a yoke which was carried on the shoulders, and from each end of which hung a rope or a chain. Pails hooked to these were easier to carry, but it was a tiring job for a child.

Although there were certain plants that yielded a soapy fluid, there was need for a supply of soap near at hand, and it was a woman's job to make it by leaching lye out of hardwood ashes and boiling it with household fats and grease. This did not make bars of soap, but a paste which was put into the water in which the clothes were washed. After soaking and, in some cases, boiling, the clothes were taken to the spring to be rinsed, wrung out, and hung to dry in sun and wind. The lye soap was kept in a small barrel into which the washer dipped on wash day.

General house cleaning was no great problem, the floors being strewn with rushes as insulation against the cold rising from the earth. When trampled, more were added, making a catch-all for dropped food which the chickens pecked up. Sweet-smelling herbs were added to the rushes, which were seldom changed and otherwise tended to smell. The hearth was swept, but there was little dusting done, since many of the household furnishings were in constant use, gathering no dust. Bedmaking was confined to airing the bedroll and stowing it out of the way. Sheets and blankets were put in the chest after use. There was wood to be stacked, water to be fetched, gardens to be tended,

ARTIFACTS SEEN IN SEVENTEENTH-CENTURY PAINTINGS

Left: **The cook at the fireplace.** *Right:* **Girl rubbing dishes at a window. Both scenes are from paintings by the Dutch artist Roghman.**

Lye & soap making

MAKING LYE AND SOAP

Lye was made by pouring water on wood ashes in a barrel. In finding its way to the bottom, the water leached out potash (potassium carbonate). This, in turn, dripped from a hole in the bottom of the barrel into a container. This liquid was boiled to concentrate it, then added to grease in a large kettle to make a crude kind of soft soap, which was put into containers for use in the household. Two or three leachings produced a liquid which was used much as a laundry bleach is today. The clothes were put in a "bucking tub" and the liquid poured over them. Next, they were "bucked," i.e., heaved around in the tub, and were taken to a stream to wash out the lye. Hung over bushes or stretched on tenterhooks, they were allowed to dry in sun and wind.

In 1751 Parliament passed an act to encourage the making of lye in the American colonies, where much more wood was available to burn.

MAKING BESOMS AND BRUSHES

Top: The besom maker compressed a bundle of birch twigs in a pinch-vise while he bound them with twine or natural vines around a handle. The handle was prevented from falling out by method *A* or *B* (see bottom part of illustration). Besoms, large and small, were used to sweep the house or paths outdoors. While not as efficient as modern brooms, the besom did a remarkably good job of sweeping. Bound twigs, without a handle, were used as pot scrubbers. The man in the background is peeling off bark with a drawknife. He also shaped the ends of the broomsticks as in *A* or *B*.

Bottom: Steps in making a brush. *C.* Frame for a brush. *D.* Side view of frame with soft grasses inserted. *E.* Completed brush, with grasses bound with twine. Such a brush had many household uses, or could be used to apply whitewash, tar, etc. to fence or boat.

and livestock to be fed and watered; these were jobs done by women and children, all of whom were useful members of the household. Babies were fed, bathed, and put to sleep; when hungry, they were breast-fed, there being no cow's milk until 1624. The family wash was done outdoors whenever possible, clothes being set to dry on fences or bushes.

SANITATION

The problem of sanitation in the colony was little different from what it was in England or Holland, both places lacking facilities that today we deem necessary to our health and well-being. Plymouth had a supply of water from springs and a nearby brook, something lacking in the Old World, and the Pilgrim village street was free of a gutter smelling of human wastes, as was not the case in the towns of Europe. Disposition of such wastes in the colony presented few difficulties. A dug pit, or "necessary" (privy), adjacent to the house sufficed for their bodily functions. In cold weather there was always the fireplace, which offered a quick way of waste disposal. As evidence that such means were used we quote advice given to a house owner about to rent his place: "Rent not your house to those who pisseth in the fireplace." Fire consumes rapidly, and who knows how many took the easy way when the temperature outdoors was below zero.

Inventories do list chamber pots, but those unearthed at Jamestown seem to be a child-size, which may indicate that children were the sole users of this handy ceramic or pewter pot. They were convenient for sudden midnight calls of nature, but often advertised too widely their contents. However, the Pilgrim nose, insensitive to the wastes of animals, would likely not be bothered by that of humans; as for body odor, this must have been ever present in the wool garments worn, but seldom washed. For that matter, the interior of a Pilgrim house must always have been redolent, with memories of the last meal cooked lingering on.

The lack of privacy in a Pilgrim house must have caused problems. This may have been one of the reasons for the erection of a partition at one end of the room; it at least hid the conjugal bed.

FURNITURE

Many Dutch prints by seventeenth-century artists depict the humble cottages of the poor, showing them cluttered with belongings stacked wherever there was room for them—on shelves, in the loft, around the room, or serving as a means of seating, as barrels often did. It is more than likely that Pilgrim houses differed little from those just mentioned, despite the fact that there were few real possessions to stow.

The Pilgrims' housekeeping tasks were greatly simplified by the paucity of furniture. Houses such as the Pilgrims built offered little in the way of comfort, but then, few were used to such. Taking the common house as typical for size, there was no room for the furniture then in style in England or Holland, nor had there been room for such in the hold of the *Mayflower*. A chest to hold clothes, a stool or two, and a bedroll were about all that each could bring aboard. In a Pilgrim house a large chest took up room on one side wall; it was opened and closed frequently during daylight hours. In it were kept the bed and table linens, plus whatever clothing was not on the backs of the various members of the family.

Chairs were scarce in the early years at Plymouth, and what few there were often served a dual purpose, having a back that could be tilted on hinges to serve as a table. Others had a straight wooden back with arms on each side and were uncomfortable for long sitting, especially since they had no cushions. "Joined" stools (joiner-made) were more common, and were backless. Stools for use at the hearth were low, sometimes with only three legs, the better to sit on the uneven stones in that area. Tables, called "boards," were just that, often just one wide plank set up on trestles. When not in use tables were stacked against a wall out of the way. The trestles were similarly stored, one on top of the other.

Pilgrim beds were not the elaborate carved versions seen in museums which feature furniture of the period. A simple bedstead consisted of a frame to which legs were affixed, the back side having a plain board incorporated to prevent the pillow-bolster from slipping off. The frame was bored with holes to take rope on which a mattress was laid. With constant use these ropes became slack, and had to be tightened by use of a bed screw. This was inserted and twisted to gather slack along the length of the frame to its end, in which there was tied a knot. This was then untied and a new knot made to prevent the rope from slipping back. The rope was threaded to form squares between the sides and ends of the frame, and on these the mattress was laid. The latter was stuffed with whatever was on hand suitable for the purpose; some stuffings used were hay, straw, cornhusks, and, later, feathers of wildfowl. Pillow cases, called pillow-beers, were stuffed likewise, and were usually of a length to fit across the width of the bed. Sheets were of coarse linen and were overlaid with blankets, even rugs when the weather was cold. Later beds were fitted with a canopy from which curtains were hung to keep out drafts. Since room was at a premium, any such bed was usually placed behind a screen built into the end of the room opposite to the fireplace. It was the custom in Holland to build bunk beds near the fireplace, but it is not known if the Pilgrims did so.

In winter the Pilgrims warmed their chilly beds with warming pans. These were brass pans, fitted with a hinged top, and equipped with a long handle made of iron (later of turned wood). The pan was receptacle for red-hot embers from the fire, forming a sort of ironing device. Holding the long handle, a housewife put the hot pan between the sheets of the bed, circling it around to give warmth to the ice-cold linen. The trick then was to quickly get into bed while the warmth lasted, hopefully to fall asleep before its comfort vanished, and let body warmth take over the task.

TOOL STORAGE

Pilgrim housekeeping arrangements were very likely similar to those found in the homes of English peasants and craftsmen of the period. In such a home, if the occupant was a craftsman, he made use of his living room as a workshop by day; seldom did he have a separate shed for such a purpose. For storage of more bulky articles, such as a plow or miscellaneous farm equipment, a shed was built against one wall of the cottage, and might double as a hen house, although chickens and sometimes pigs had the run of the house. In Pilgrim houses it is

more than likely that the open area to one side of the fireplace was used to stack garden tools, unless the house had a lean-to for this purpose. Old prints show space between the ceiling rafters slatted to take long-handled tools. Some articles, such as a baby's cradle, were in constant use; a cradle would be difficult to stow, but it may have been accepted as necessary clutter.

A carpenter seldom cleaned up his shavings, since they mixed with the rushes laid over the floor as insulation. His larger chips would serve as kindling for the fire, as would board ends too short to be used.

LAMPS AND TORCHES

The Pilgrims customarily went to bed with the sun and rose at dawn to continue their labors. On those rare occasions when they did venture forth at night, they may have used pine knots, easily obtainable from local trees, as a source of light. These knots, full of rich sap, provided a smoky light when lit. Many of the castles in the Old World, as the Pilgrims knew, had fitted in their walls rings in which such knots could be set, burning for a considerable time to light stairways and dark passages. In the event a ship came to shore at night, pine knots could be emplaced on shore in a cresset, a basketlike device set on a pole, to guide in the crew. Old prints show burning pine knots being carried in a portable cresset by a night watchman.

As for indoor lighting devices, they were scarce among the Pilgrims. Candles were expensive and were used mostly in lanterns, not many of which are found in inventories of the period. Instead, use was made of oils and grease set in a bowllike device called a crusie. A flax wick set in the oil was lit to provide light. Another source of light were rushes of the species *Juncus conglomeratus,* which has a pithy core. These were peeled of their outer skin and soaked in kitchen grease in a "grisset" placed on the hearth. They were then set in a rushlight holder, a pincerlike device of iron, set into a wooden stand. This rush, when lighted at both ends gave rise to the saying "burning the candle at both ends," something which is not possible with a candle set in a candlestick. The rushlight was in use in England until late in the nineteenth century, and

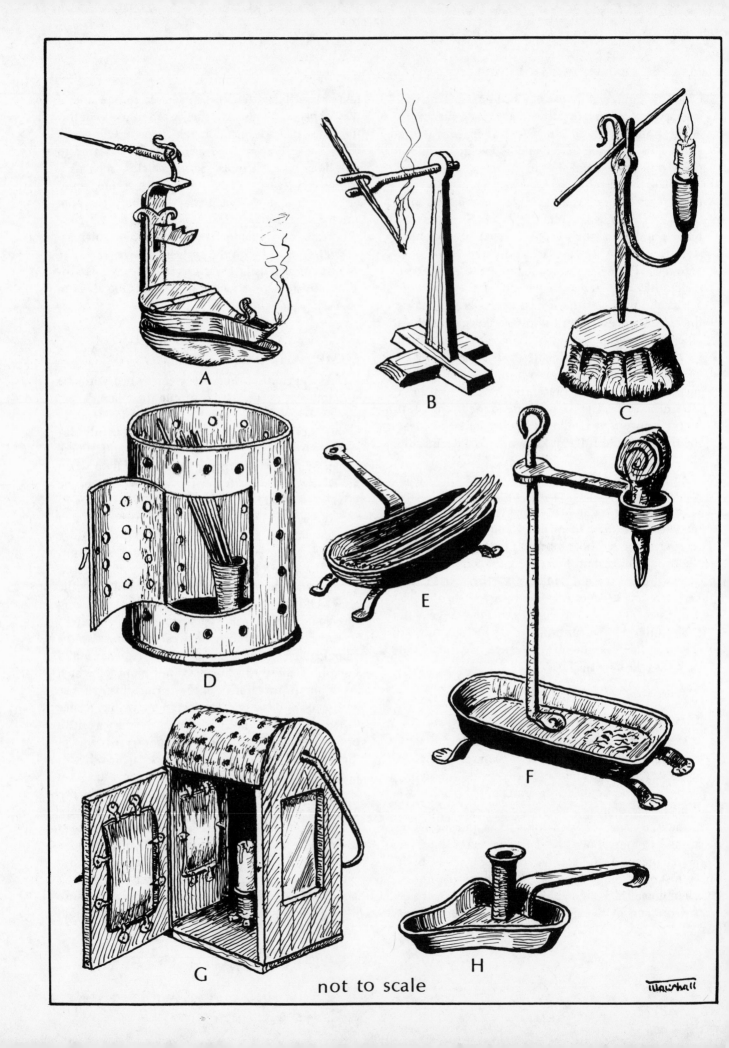

A

B

C

D

E

F

G

H

not to scale

is mentioned in Gilbert White's *Natural History and Antiquities of Selborne,* wherein its preparation is described in some detail as an occupation of the very poor, who prepared rushlights for richer households. When all is said and done, however, undoubtedly the major source of indoor illumination for the Pilgrims was the fire on the hearth.

HOUSE MAINTENANCE

Besides their many housekeeping chores, the Pilgrims faced the task of maintaining their houses in good condition. Of necessity, the Pilgrim householder lavished much attention on his chimney. When summer rolled around it was possible to cook outdoors, the chimney was inspected for bare spots where clay may have fallen away from the wattle. Chimneys were large, and inspecting them was a dirty job. It was important to keep the chimneys intact, free from grease where a spark could catch and smolder, then burst into flame as it reached the dry underside of the thatch. Besides chimneys other parts of houses and fences required replacement with the passage of time. The palisade would tend to rot where the posts were buried in the ground, and this meant a trip to the woods to cut replacement poles and posts. The fort was subject to rot, as Bradford records, eventually leading to the building of a new and better one.

Pilgrim Arms and Armor

In regard to their arms and armor the Pilgrims would have been much better off if they had left most of it back in England. Not only was the armor heavy, but it was hot in summer and snagged on trees and bushes. Besides, the Pilgrims had no enemy to face after they made peace with the In-dians. They discarded this impedimenta except perhaps during special occasions or when raiding places such as Merrymount, where they faced musket shots (see chapter 10). The pikes and halberds were of no value in the colony, unless they converted them to other use. These were weapons for staged battles in which cavalry had to be faced, the pikes presenting a spiked barricade against the horses. The firearms the Pilgrims brought were the best available at that time, but better weapons were shortly to be introduced. The blunderbuss, so often shown in Pilgrim pictures, did not come into use until the end of the seventeenth century. The cannon mounted on the fort were the best of their day, but saw little use in Plymouth. They were, however, a useful means of frightening any Indians with plans to attack the village. An armorer came to Plymouth on one of the later ships, and was employed full-time keeping the colony's firearms in good condition. Standish, as a military man, had a collection of firearms, including some of the more advanced type, but these gave trouble, mainly because they had to be wound before firing, often resulting in a broken spring. Steel was inferior in these times, and even the best of armorers found iron hard to make into steel that would hold a temper.

PILGRIM CLOTHING

The Pilgrims, especially those who spent much time in the woods, had more trouble keeping their clothing intact than they did in maintaining their houses and firearms in good condition. Under their agreement with their backers the Pilgrims had to purchase all their supplies through the company, and so they did no spinning, weaving, tailoring, or cobbling. By the time their friends arrived from

EARLY LIGHTING DEVICES

A. Crusie. This consisted of two iron pans. The top one, with hinged cover, contained oil and a wick, and was removable for filling. The lower pan caught the drips. The crusie could be suspended from a hook, or be hung from a spike driven into wood. *B.* Wood splint holder. A sliver of fatty wood was set in the forked crosspiece and ignited. *C.* Combination candle and rushlight holder. Certain pithy rushes were peeled, leaving a strip of peel as a support. These were soaked in kitchen grease in a grisset *(E).* In use the rushlight was placed in the pincerlike holder, the weight of the candleholder pinching it tight. *D.* Rushlight lantern. This was one of the earliest forms of indoor lantern. A cup held the rushlights, only one of which was burned; the rest were spares. Placed on table or shelf, it gave enough light to banish darkness. *E.* Iron grisset. Besides its use in soaking rushlights, it was placed under a roast to catch dripping grease. *F.* Pine-knot holder. The fatty knots of conifers burned with a smoky flame but gave more light than candle or rushlight. *G.* Wooden lantern with pierced metal top. Windows were of horn, giving rise to the term "lanthorne." *H.* Combination crusie and candlestick.

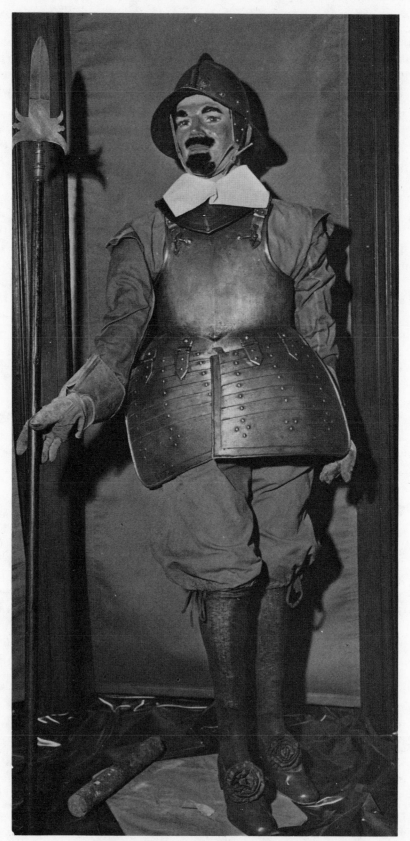

EARLY SEVENTEENTH-CENTURY ARMOR

The armor shown is typical of that worn by the Pilgrims of Plymouth, who were quick to discard it. Featured are a morion (helmet), breastplate, and corselet. The helmet, last to be discarded, was abandoned after King Philip's War (1675-78). The halberd and pike were also discarded as weapons.— *Photograph by Randall W. Abbott*

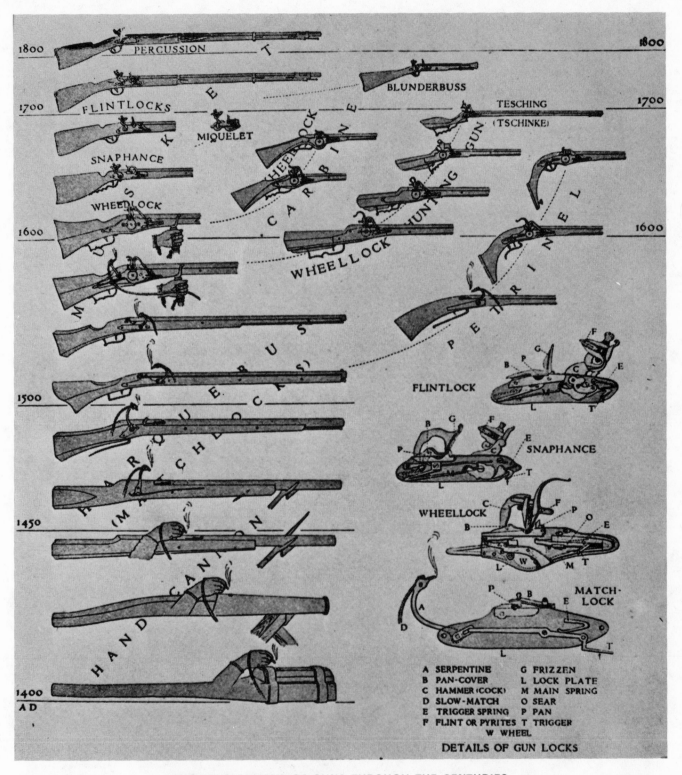

THE DEVELOPMENT OF GUNS THROUGH THE CENTURIES

As may be seen, the blunderbuss, so often shown in illustrations of the Pilgrims, was not developed at the time of their arrival at Plymouth. Their most common weapon was the matchlock, although Myles Standish, their military leader, may have owned a wheellock or a snaphance, which were quicker to fire. Shown are the mechanisms of the various guns.

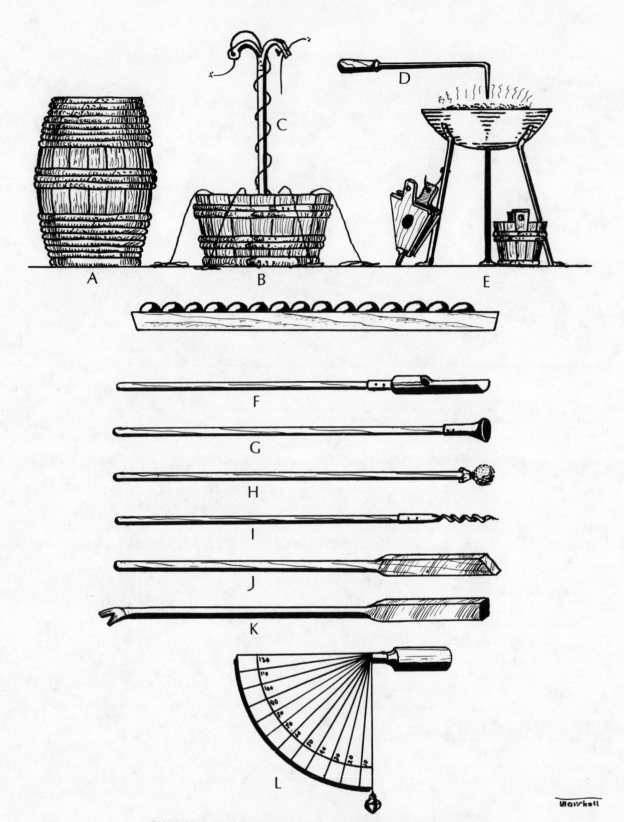

GUNNER'S EQUIPMENT OF THE SEVENTEENTH CENTURY

A. Gunpowder barrel, stoutly bound with wooden staves. Iron hoops were never used because of the danger of sparks which might ignite the powder. *B.* Fuse tub, filled with sand, in which is set a linstock *(C).* The head of the linstock holds the match or fuse. Alternate methods of holding the match are shown: on the left, the fuse is pulled through a hole; on the right, the fuse is held by a small screw-vise. A series of lighted fuses were set around the tub during the time a cannon was in use. The fuses were made by soaking three-strand twine in nitre, which made it slow-burning. *E.* Charcoal brazier holding live coals for heating the match or touch-hole prick *(D),* which was kept red-hot during action. The long trough holds the iron balls which are fired from the cannon. *F.* Gunpowder scoop, made slightly smaller in diameter than the bore of the cannon. The scoop fed gunpowder down the barrel. This was followed by a retainer wad of cloth. *G.* Ramrod for forcing home the retainer wad. A ball followed the wad down the barrel. *H.* Swab or sponge for cleaning out the barrel after the gun was fired. *I.* Cleaning screw for reaming caked powder from the gunbarrel. *J.* Wooden handspike for moving the gun carriage into position. *K.* Iron crowbar, for the same purpose. *L.* Gunner's quadrant, fitted in the muzzle of the gun to determine its elevation in degrees of angle when firing at a distant target.

The Musket and its equipment

THE MUSKET AND ITS EQUIPMENT

Top: The musket in firing position, supported on a linstock. Slung round the gunner's shoulder is a bandolier, from which his charging powder cylinders, each containing one charge, are suspended on thongs. The caps are left off after they are emptied down the gun barrel. After charging his musket with powder the gunner rams a wad of cloth down the barrel to retain the charge. He then drops a lead ball in and fires by squeezing the lever under the musket. This brings the serpentine holding his lighted match (fuse) over the flash-pan on the side of the gun. If the charge ignites, it in turn ignites the charge in the barrel, and this propels the ball towards its target.

Bottom: A. Two types of flash-powder flasks, made of wood, leather-covered, and decorated with brass binding. The spring-loaded catch controlled the amount of powder poured into the flash-pan and helped keep the powder dry. *B.* Iron bullet mold (shown open). When the mold was closed, lead poured through a hole in its side formed a round ball. *C.* Lighted match carrier. This perforated tube was carried on the belt, with a lighted match inside. It was important always to have a lighted match (fuse) ready to place in the serpentine of the musket. *D.* Close-up of gunpowder cylinder carried on the bandolier. It was turned from wood and suspended on a cord so it could not get lost.

The musket was far from being a good hunting gun, being slow to load, and dependent on dry powder to fire. Sometimes the gunner would get a "flash in the pan" if the hole from the flash-pan into the barrel was clogged. Also, the musket was heavy and had to be supported during firing. Yet it remained a favorite with the Pilgrims, being often more reliable than the more modern wheellock musket, the spring of which frequently broke in action, rendering the gun useless. The flintlock musket was a more reliable gun, but was late in reaching the American colonies.

MUSKETEERS FIRING A VOLLEY

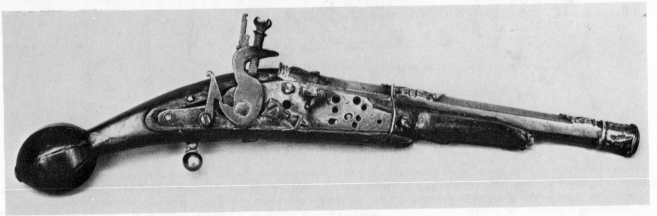

DOG-LOCK PISTOL

This type of flintlock was named for the little dog catch that kept the pistol at half-cock until ready to fire. It is now preserved in Pilgrim Hall, Plymouth, Massachusetts.—*Photograph courtesy of Pilgrim Hall*

England, the colonists were clad in rags, with "patches on patches," as is recorded. Some of the more handy people may have fashioned jackets from the skins of animals but, even so, how replace worn-out undergarments? Unlike their Indian friends the colonists could not run around half-naked, nor would their modesty have let them. The Pilgrims had been shocked at the first sight of Samoset as he strode into their village half naked.

Because of a lack of pictures showing costumes worn by the class from which most of the Pilgrims came, it is difficult to say with any assurance what they wore. Many came from East Anglia on the east coast of England, an area in close contact with Holland. There was a strong Dutch influence over that part of the country. Moreover, the Pilgrims had lived in Leyden, and may well have adopted current Dutch fashions in dress, to some degree. Hollar, an artist of the period, made many drawings in England which showed the prevailing dress of both sexes, and these much resemble those we are accustomed to see in pictures of the Pilgrims.

Men wore baggy breeches, tied with a cord at the knee, below which they covered their legs with thick woolen hose. Shoes were of simple design, square-toed, and tied with a leather thong. Both shoes were made on the same last, so there was no left and right fit. Men wore a loose-fitting linen shirt with full sleeves, tucked into the top of their breeches, which were held up by a tied string. Over the shirt it was customary to wear a jerkin, sometimes of leather but usually of wool. It was often made without sleeves, which were fashioned separately and could be fitted by lacing at the shoulders. This joint was hidden by an overlapping shoulder-piece. Headgear was a tall-crowned felt hat with a wide brim. When doing physical labor men wore a stocking cap (Monmouth cap), or one of tufted wool called a "thrum" cap, also worn at sea by sailors.

Women wore long woolen skirts, under which were several petticoats and undergarments of linen. Blouses were full-cut in both bodice and sleeves. Around the neck the women wore a scarf, made to hang down the back with a pointed effect. Over the head was wrapped a snood which passed under the chin. The tall hat was worn on top of this, but in-doors a linen cap was substituted. Shoes were simple, and much the same as for men, but of softer leather. When walking on muddy streets pattens were worn. These were wooden platforms tied to the feet with thongs. They elevated the feet and the hems of skirts above the mud. Children dressed in smaller replicas of adult clothes, the girls wearing pinafores over their skirts.

Far from looking drab, the Pilgrims wore colorful clothes, unlike their neighbors of the Massachusetts Bay Colony, who wore black. Pilgrim colors were obtained from natural dyes, made from plants or lichens, which produced mulberry, brown, yellow, and blue. Some of the Pilgrim leaders wore capes of red and purple, colors that were usually made from exotic dyes from the Orient. These capes must have originated in Holland, since it is doubtful if any plants known to the Pilgrims could produce such colors. Some of the drawings mentioned above show both men and women wearing ruffs and starched cuffs. There may have been some among the colonists who wore these, but the problems of laundering and pleating point to their limited use, as perhaps in church or courtroom. Cooks may have worn oversleeves to protect their everyday garments during food preparation, but it is more likely that they pulled up their sleeves; hence their fullness of cut. Aprons were worn but, because of the proximity of the fire during cooking operations, the women pulled up their skirts, tucking them in at the waist. When sitting on a stool at the hearth, it was an easy matter to pull the skirts up over the knees, even though this exposed the bare legs to the heat of the fire.

Outdoor garments were not common, except for a cape; a long overcoat would hamper a man engaged in work in the woods, where he stripped for action to his shirt and breeches. When a man got cold, he donned more garments under his shirt. If Pilgrim women had time to knit, their men may have worn a woolen undergarment. Mittens were worn rather than gloves, which only the rich could afford. Long boots were not uncommon in the colony, particularly for hunting in the marshes.

Whether in the matter of clothing, furniture, tools, or utensils, the Pilgrims did not possess an abundance of worldly goods, as their wills and in-

DRESS OF THE PILGRIMS AND THEIR CONTEMPORARIES

Pictures of seventeenth-century English dress, other than that worn by the rich, are hard to come by since artists of the day, with the exception of the Dutch, did not often depict the working class. What few pictures there are were printed in the *Roxburgh Ballads,* a book issued in several volumes during the seventeenth century. The costume of the common people changed very little for two centuries, and what influence there was for change came into England via Holland. The dress of the Pilgrims was like that of the Dutch since East Anglia, whence some of them came, was peopled by artisans who came to England from Holland to work in the wool industry. Illustrated here are typical costumes of the sixteenth and seventeenth centuries: *A.* Field laborer, from the *Roxburgh Ballads. B.* Typical dress of a Pilgrim field laborer at Plymouth. *C.* Milkmaid of the seventeenth century (typical dress of a Pilgrim of Plymouth). *D.* Woman field hand (typical dress of a Pilgrim of Plymouth). *E.* Woman returning from market, from a sixteenth-century print. *F.* Woman's costume of the seventeenth century. *G.* Woman at spinning wheel, from a seventeenth-century print.

ventories reveal. To give an idea of what a typical inventory contained, here is one left by Myles Standish, who died at Duxbury in October 1656.

MYLES STANDISH'S INVENTORY

Item—4 oxen
   ″ —2 mares to mare coults one young horse
   ″ —six cowes 3 heifers and one calfe
   ″ —8 ewe sheep two rames and one wether
   ″ —14 swine great and smale

   ″ —one fouling peece 3 musketts 4 carbines 2 smale guns one old barrell
   ″ —one sword one cutles 3 belts
   ″ —the history of the world and the turkish history
   ″ —a Cronicle of England and the countrey ffarmer
   ″ —ye history of queen Ellisabeth and state of Europe Vusebious Dodines earball
   ″ —Doctor halls workes Calvins Institutions

" —Wilcocks workes and Mayors

" —rogers seaven treatises and the ffrench Akadamey

" —3 old bibles

" —Cecers Comentaryes Bariffes artillery

" —Prestons Sermons Burroughes Christian contentment gosspell Conversation passions of the mind the Phisitions practice Burrowghes earthly mindednes Burroughs Descovery

" —Ball on faith Brinssleys watch Dod on the lords Supper Sparke against herisye Davenports apollogye

" —a reply to Doctor Cotten on baptisme the Garmen history the Sweden Intelligencer reasons Discused

" —1 Testament one Psalme booke Nature and grace in Conflict a law booke the mean in mourning allegation against B P of Durham Johnson against hearing

" —a prcell of old bookes of Divers subjects in quarto

" —an other prcell in Octavo

" —Wilsons Dixonary homers Illiads a Comentary on James balls Cattechesmes

" —halfe a young heiffer

DRESS OF THE PILGRIMS AND THEIR CONTEMPORARIES *(cont.)*

A. Shepherds, from a series of prints on trades (1642). *B.* Shepherd shearing a sheep, from a seventeenth-century print. *C.* Sailor of the seventeenth century. *D.* Water carrier, from a contemporary print (1623). *E.* Mother and child, from a seventeenth-century Dutch painting. *F.* Drayman, from a book on trades (1679). *G.* Man in cape (seventeenth century). *H.* Male dress, from the *Roxburgh Ballads.*

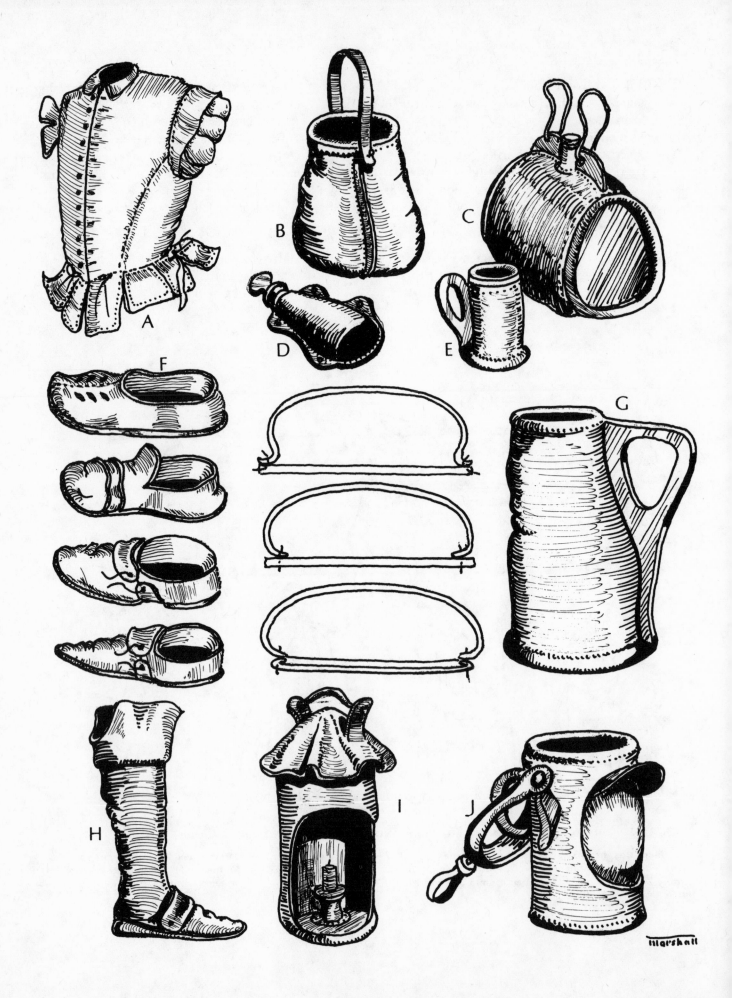

'' —one feather bed bolster and 2 pillowes
'' —1 blankett a Coverlid and a rugg
'' —1 feather bed blankett and great pillow
'' —one old featherbed
'' —one feather bed and bolster
'' —one blankett and 2 ruggs
'' —one feather bolster and old rugg
'' —4 paire of fine sheets
'' —1 Tablecloth 4 napkins
'' —his wearing clothes
'' —16 peeces of pewter
'' —earthen ware
'' —3 brasse kettles one skillett
'' —4 Iron potts
'' —a warming pan a frying pan and a Cullender
'' —one paire of stillyeards*
'' —2 bedsteds one table forme Chaires 1 Chest and 2 boxes
'' —1 bedsted one settle bed one box 3 caske
'' —1 bedsted 3 Chists 3 Casses with som bottles 1 box 4 caske
'' —one Still
'' —1 old settle 1 Chaire one kneading trough 2 pailes 2 traies one Dozen of trenchers 1 bowle 1 ferkin 1 beer Caske and 1 Table
'' —2 beer Caske 1 Chern 2 spining wheels one powdering tubb† 2 old Caske one old flaskett
'' —one mault mill
'' —2 sawes with Divers Carpenters tooles
'' —a Timber Chaine with plow Chaines

'' —2 saddles a pillion 1 bridle
'' —old iron
'' —1 Chist and a buckin Tubb‡
'' —1 hachell§ 2 tramells 2 Iron Doggs 1 spitt one fierforke 1 lamp 2 gars one lanthorn with other old lumber
'' —in woole
'' —hemp and flax
'' —eleven bushells of wheat
'' —14 bushells of rye
'' —30 bushells of pease
'' —25 bushells of Indian Corn
'' —Cart and yeokes and plow Irons and 1 brake
'' —axes sickles hookes and other tooles
'' —eight Iron hoopes 1 spining wheele with other lumber

From this inventory of a prominent Pilgrim it may be seen that he had few worldly goods to show for his years in the colony; other wills and inventories are similar in content. Inventories are an important source of information about the Pilgrims possessions because much of their everyday equipment, being of wood, rotted before archaeologists could excavate. These inventories seem skimpy, since much of what was used in daily life was not considered valuable enough to include in an inventory. This may make some wonder why "old iron" appears in the Standish inventory. Iron was a scarce commodity which could be recycled, and

---

*Steelyards. A steelyard was a type of scale dating back to Roman times. It was surprisingly accurate, and consisted of a long arm with a sliding weight. In use the scale was hung by a hook and the object to be weighed placed on a hook on the scale. By sliding the weight along the graduated arm until a balance was achieved, the weight was read off the scale.

†A tub in which meat was put and powdered with salt to preserve it for winter use.

‡A bucking tub was a tub used for bleaching during the dyeing process.

§A hackle was a tool set with spikes and used for combing flax before spinning.

LEATHERWORK

A. Doublet of buff leather, in which the sections are joined with butt seams (late sixteenth century). **B.** Leather fire bucket (sixteenth century). **C.** Costrel of molded leather. This was a leather bottle used to carry liquids into the fields. **D.** Flacklet or flask of molded leather, with eyelets for securing to the belt. **E.** Blackjack or drinking mug, with silver mount around its top. Its interior is lined with black pitch. **F.** Shoes. The top two are sixteenth-century; the bottom two, seventeenth-century. The bottom one is for a woman. To the right are three ways in which uppers were sewn to soles with waxed thread. **G.** Great bombard (five-gallon capacity), a serving jug for ale. Its interior is lined with black pitch, which did not flavor the contents. **H.** Seventeenth-century high boot. This was not necessarily a riding boot, but was used when in the field, or wading a stream. **I** and **J.** Two "leathern lanthornes." The one on the right has a horn window. These lanterns were in use from medieval times.—*Artifacts in the collections of the Museum of Leathercraft, Walsall, England*

with which broken tools could be repaired. With a source of supply over 3,000 miles away, nothing was hastily discarded. Another likely reason for the incompleteness of Pilgrim inventories is that some tools probably were held in common and therefore appear on no list. It should also be kept in mind that the town of Plymouth was built over the site of the original Pilgrim village at a time when there was little or no interest in Pilgrim artifacts, which may still lie buried in places impossible to excavate. Thus we may be shortchanging the Pilgrims, not knowing what they had in their houses. It must be pointed out, however, that excavated sites of later Pilgrim houses did not reveal too much in the way of the better things one would expect of the more prosperous Pilgrims who made it big in cattle. Pilgrim Hall*, a museum devoted to telling the Pilgrim story, has a few artifacts that were supposedly handed down in Pilgrim families, but there are few enough of these. One can only marvel that the Pilgrims built a thriving colony with so little in the way of material goods.

*in Plymouth, Massachusetts

Chapter 7

Pilgrim Medicine

IN the seventeenth century, a winter Atlantic voyage would tax a person of most robust constitution; confined below deck in constant dampness, with few facilities for cooking or for human needs, this person would suffer. Probable seasickness would cause the body to lose heat and the nutrients of any food vomited. There were those who made such voyages, mainly fishermen sailing to Newfoundland, but they tried to pick a time when storms were fewer, and the going less rough. The Pilgrims from Leyden, and others who joined them before departure, would suffer on such a voyage from sickness, coughs, and colds. Some may have harbored the bacilli of tuberculosis, which would incubate during the trip, then manifest their virulence in a galloping form, quickly finishing off the victims. While some medical authorities think the sickness suffered at Plymouth may have been consumption, as it was then called, others favor typhus or smallpox as the villain. Since doctor Fuller

kept no medical logbook, we do not even have his opinion on what the disease was that took the lives of half the colonists in the first few months; nor did Giles Heale, surgeon on the *Mayflower*, voice his opinion.

Typhus, then called gaol fever, was caused by the bites of fleas that infested the rodents to be found in gaols, and aboard ships. The *Mayflower* was accounted a sweet ship, as far as her bilge was concerned, but that area of the ship must have housed rats. Thus, it is possible some of the passengers may have come down with typhus. Lacking fresh meat and fresh fruit or vegetables, some may have developed scurvy. The fishermen who were in contact with Indians in New England brought over diseases, and one of these almost wiped out the Indians of Plymouth. When the working party went ashore, many got sick at once, giving rise to the theory that they were struck down by the same disease that carried off the Indians.

Medical authorities cannot agree on the nature of the disease or diseases that afflicted the colonists; the possibilities are listed above. Whatever diseases the Pilgrims had, they proved fatal to many, and complicated matters for the leaders of the colony. It is noteworthy, though, that many of those who did survive lived to a ripe age, even though the colony suffered several epidemics over the years.*

Both Bradford and Carver fell sick, and lay abed in the common house. The Pilgrims' troubles multiplied as workers fell sick, some dying within hours.† The common house was filled from wall to wall with bedrolls, as the sickness became general. Here is how Bradford described the situation:

So as there died some times two or three of a day in the fore said time, that of 100 and odd persons, scarce fifty remained. And of these, in the time of most distress, there was but six or seven sound persons who to their great commendations be it spoken, spared no pains night and day, but with abundance of toil, and hazard of their own health, fetched them wood, made them fires, dressed them meat, made their beds, washed their loathsome clothes, clothed and unclothed them. In a word, did all the homely and necessary offices for them which dainty and queasy stomachs cannot endure to hear named . . .

In this description Bradford offers no clues as to the nature of the sickness from which many of the colonists suffered. There is no mention of eruptions on the body, such as occur in cases of typhus or the plague. We do not know if the clothing of those sick was made "loathsome" by vomit, diarrhea, or blood from tubercular lungs. As Bradford remarked, just to think of such things is distasteful for those with a queasy stomach. The disease must have had great psychological impact, coming as it did on top of a wretched voyage. One victim went out of his head, cursing those who tended him, but repented just before he died.

Bradford saw the sickness of the Pilgrims, which

spared many of their leaders, as a trial sent to test their faith. Brewster and Standish were among those who stayed healthy, but Rose, wife of Standish died. Both these Pilgrim leaders were of yeoman stock, and of a sturdier constitution than others who had joined the venture at the time the congregation came over from Leyden. Others too, with a country background, must have been robust enough to survive in a land which demanded the most from a person.

Although the *Mayflower* carried a surgeon, Giles Heale, Bradford does not mention the part he played during the sickness. It is hard to believe that, under the circumstances, he would hold himself aloof from the sick; yet the barber-surgeon was seldom called to the bedside of a patient unless there was need for the knife. It was the physician who was called for everyday sickness, and he had an array of drugs and medicines in his bag, one of which he would prescribe as he saw fit. Samuel Fuller, the physician to the colonists, worked hard and long during the prevailing sickness. It is unlikely that he had any drug which could save the life of any of his patients. Even today, the Pilgrims' disease, whatever it was, might be a challenge to a doctor, but physicians nowadays have a wider variety of drugs with which to work.

MEDICAL KNOWLEDGE OF THE SEVENTEENTH CENTURY

It is not unlikely that the leaders of the colony all had some knowledge of medicine. Those who had attended a university would be familiar with translations of Greek works on medicine and botany recently rediscovered by scholars, and printed and circulated among the principal seats of learning in Europe. In fact, medical theory of the seventeenth century was based on the works of Galen (A.D. 130-201), who had gathered together the writings of others to compile his book. Those taking holy orders at the university were required to read these books and, when ordained, make use of the knowledge contained in them to deal with sickness in the parish. Brewster was such a person, and he would have been able to assist doctor Fuller and, in addition, minister to the sick and comfort them in their dying moments.

---

*John Alden, the last survivor of the signers of the Mayflower Compact, lived to be eighty-nine, surviving his wife Priscilla by some thirty years. Brewster and Allerton both made their three score and ten years, and Bradford was but two years short of that mark when he died.
†Of the 102 passengers who reached Cape Cod, 4 died before the ship anchored at Plymouth; and by the summer of 1621 half their number died. This made necessary a reshuffling of families, children whose parents had died being put with a family, which would also contain unmarried males and females. The ship served as a home for all until sufficient housing was built for them to move ashore.

PHYSICIAN AND SURGEON

In the late sixteenth century the physician and the surgeon dressed alike.—*Print of 1588*

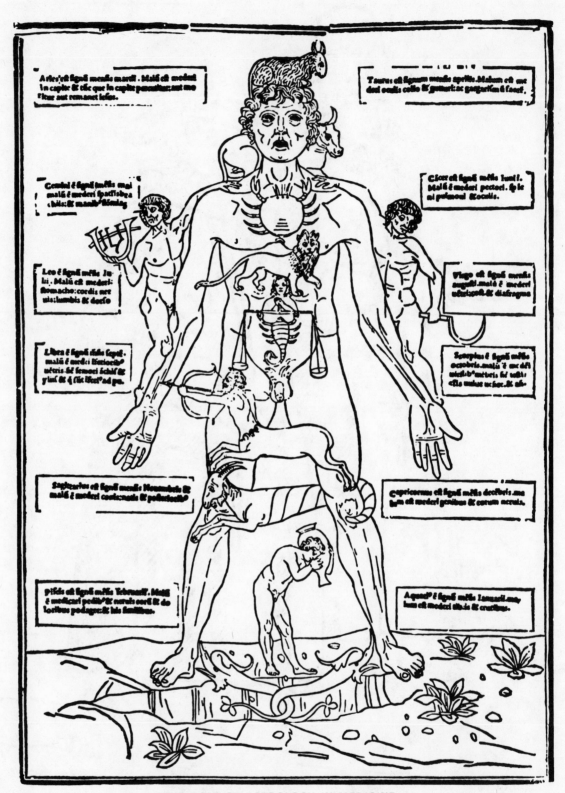

THE ROLE OF ASTROLOGY IN MEDICINE

This illustration from *Faciculus Medicinae* by Johannes De Ketham, published in Venice in 1513, shows the supposed influence of the planets on the human body.

At this point, it seems appropriate to set forth the state of medicine as it was practiced in the late sixteenth century and early into the next. For centuries the sick had been at the mercy of witchcraft and its practitioners. Astrology was looked upon as a means of discovering which planets were responsible for a person's sickness, in relation to the month of birth. Unscientific cures were brewed from herbs and chemicals; it was a kill-or-cure situation. Thus it was that when the works of Galen became better known, the situation changed to some degree, except that astrology still played a part in diagnosing the sickness of a patient. The newly published herbals offered a whole range of new medicines, made from herbs common in most gardens.

The Theories of Galen

The physicians of the day, mostly university-trained, took Galen's medical theories to heart. These were based on the premise that there were four elements in the world—fire, water, air, and earth—and four primary qualities—warm, cold, moist, and dry—corresponding to the four fluids—blood, phlegm, yellow bile, and black bile. The secondary qualities perceptible to the physician were the result of a variable mixture of the elements. They were taste, smell, hardness or softness, wet or cold, and warmth or dryness. A doctor was required to have some knowledge of human anatomy, and this was made easier to learn by the publication of a book based on dissections made by artists and medical students at the University of Padua, then a great seat of learning. Such practices as the dissection of human corpses were frowned on by church authorities, and had to be performed in secret.

Galenic practitioners, even armed with a knowledge of anatomy, physiology, and the use of herbs, were of little use to patients suffering from epidemic diseases. They had no weapons with which to fight germs, as does the doctor today. Furthermore, most physicians, being of the upper class, treated only those of their own kind. The poor had to go to the apothecary for their nostrums. Further down the medical scale were the barber-surgeons. Little better than butchers, they had scant training, and were only visited as a last resort. Today, the roles of surgeon and physican are reversed, the surgeon being regarded as the top man in his profession.

The Theories of Paracelsus

Like most professions medicine had its dissenters, and early in the seventeenth century there were doctors who rejected Galenic theories in favor of those of Paracelsus (1493-1541), who believed that nature was the best healer. He advised restraint in the treatment of wounds, which would heal themselves if left alone. He advised the use of surgery only as a last recourse, despite the fact that more was known about human anatomy after Vesalius published his book on the subject in the late sixteenth century. Whether from his knowledge of the human body or for other reasons, Vesalius was opposed to the theories of Galen and the superstitions surrounding the practice of medicine, which still clung to astrology as a diagnostic tool.

Herbals

Just what school Fuller subscribed to is not known, but it is more than likely that he was partial to Galen and, being out of touch with new ideas then becoming prevalent in Europe, remained ignorant of them. Fuller probably had in his possession one of the herbals then in print, either that of Gerard or the later editions of others in that field. He did not have that of Culpeper, probably the most well known, since it was not yet published (Culpeper was born in 1616). Gerard, who had studied medicine, was employed as superintendent of gardens for one of Queen Elizabeth's ministers, Lord Burleigh. These gardens contained over 1,000 specimens of plants, which Gerard described in his herbal, listing the properties of each and the various illnesses each was good for. His book was not in Latin, but in the vernacular, so that anyone who could read could learn from it. Later, Gerard opened his own apothecary shop. By charging the rich high prices for his nostrums, he was able to let the poor have them free, or at low cost. The doctors did not like Gerard, who, in their opinion, betrayed

WOODCUT FROM *RARIORUM PLANTARUM HISTORIA*

Charles de l'Ecluse (Carolus Clusius), the imperial gardener to Emperor Maximilian II and the father of descriptive botany, published his encyclopedic work, *Rariorum Plantarum Historia,* in 1609. It gave a full account of the known plant world. Many other herbalists and botanists of the Renaissance and after—most notably Clusius' contemporary, John Gerard—freely borrowed from Clusius' remarkably detailed and beautiful woodcuts for their own works.

them by writing his book in English, rather than Latin, which would have preserved their secrets.

The Training of Physicians

From time to time efforts were made to upgrade the practice of medicine and improve the training of doctors. Henry VIII had granted charters to the barber-surgeons, and a school was set up to train them in better practices. Ambroise Paré (1510-1590) was a prominent French surgeon, with much experience in the treatment of wounds received in battle. He wrote a book in the vernacular which was widely read by those training to be surgeons. In 1518 the Royal College of Physicians had been organized by Thomas Linacre, who published a code of conduct for doctors. Conditions were getting better in the medical profession, but there was still a long way to go before doctors were well enough equipped in knowledge and technique to perform delicate operations without fear of the patient dying on the operating table.

COMMONLY PRESCRIBED REMEDIES

It is doubtful if Doctor Fuller ever had to

from old prints

EXAMINATION OF URINE IN THE SIXTEENTH CENTURY

This practice lasted well into the seventeenth century although doctors were not yet equipped to use urine as a disease indicator.

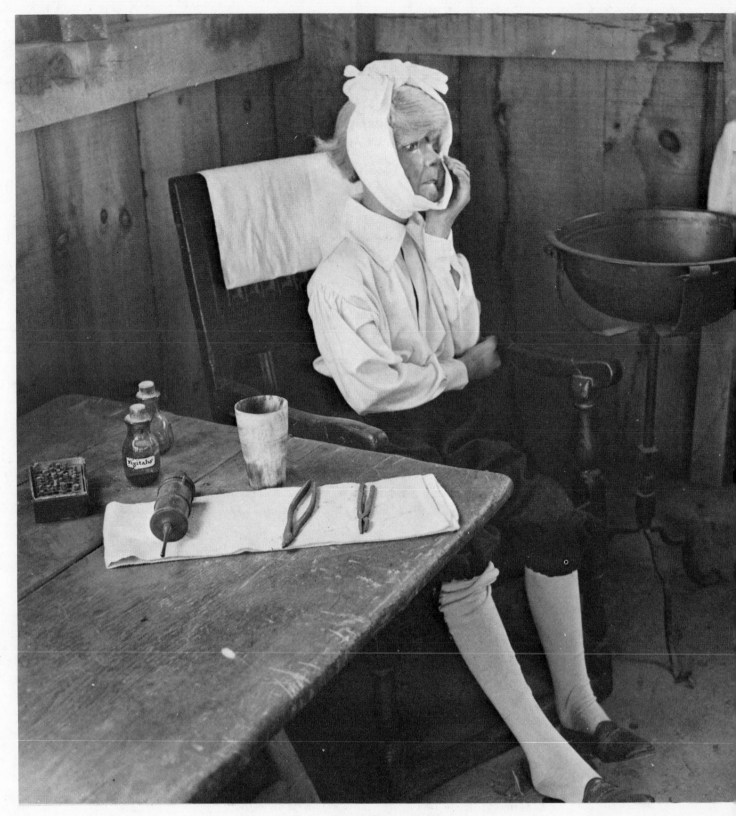

PILGRIM DENTISTRY

A Pilgrim boy awaits the attention of Doctor Fuller. On the table are dental instruments used in the seventeenth century.

perform a serious operation. Bradford mentions none and, outside of severe cuts and broken bones, he avoided surgery, which he knew he was not competent to perform. His remedies were those prescribed for the common illnesses of the times. These included plague, syphilis, typhus, and smallpox. For these most doctors prescribed rest, fresh air, and massage, knowing full well they had no cures for most of them. Some doctors were partial to bloodletting for various ills. Doctor Fuller made use of this practice, as the records show. There was also the taking of urine samples; this practice is known to us from paintings, in which a doctor is shown holding the urine flask up to the light. References to bloodletting and urine sampling appear in plays by Shakespeare. In Richard II he has this to say:

Let's purge this choler without letting blood. Our doctors say this is no month to bleed.

This quote indicates the doctor's dependence on astrology, with the patient obviously not in line with the right planet. Shakespeare refers to the examination of urine, at least by its color, in *Henry IV:*

He said, sir, the water itself was a good healthy water; but, for the party that owed it, he might have more diseases than he knew for.

Again, in *Two Gentlemen of Verona:*

These follies are within you and shine through you like the water in a urinal, that not an eye that sees you but is a physician to comment on your malady.

These quotations by a keen observer of the times serve to give us some idea of the medical situation as it existed then.

Had Doctor Fuller kept a journal of his medical practice, with notes on his treatment for various ailments, we should be in a better position to assess his merits as a doctor. With the departure of surgeon Heale on the *Mayflower,* Fuller was on his own. He was the first doctor to practice in New England and, from what accounts we have of him, he seems to have been highly respected, not only at Plymouth but in colonies that were established at Boston and along the coast beyond. Fuller's wife, who had not accompanied him on the voyage to the New World, came out on the *Swan* in 1623, assisting her husband in the capacity of nurse and midwife, which

latter practice she followed for many years after the death of her husband from smallpox in 1633.

Drugs and Herbs

Among the drugs to be found in medical chests of seventeenth-century physicians were crocus metalorum, rosin of jalap, and venice treacle—all used to induce sweating, purging, and vomiting. Powdered snakeroot was used as a diuretic and to treat gout and rheumatism. Dittany was prescribed for worms and to induce sweating. Other staples of the seventeenth-century medicine kit were molasses, Saint-John's-wort, comfrey, hartshorn (ammonia), rose hips, and sassafras. The latter was a cure-all prescribed for dysentery, skin diseases, and syphilis. It went out of use at the end of the century. A list dated 1618 includes the following pharmaceuticals: angelica, anise, lemon balm, basil, wild beet, camphor, cinnamon, cardamom, corn oil, gillyflowers, elder, honeywort, lily (madonna), mint, parsley, peppermint, pine oil (oil of turpentine), syrup of rose hips, scorpionwort, tarragon, thistle, wildwood, and wormwood.

Since there are no records of drugs supplied to the colony, we must assume that the Pilgrims made use of herbs as medicine. (Nonmedical uses of herbs by the Pilgrims were covered in chapter 6.) The old herbalists were prone to advertise various of their herbs by citing their properties, thus:

Basil—sowen in gardens in earthen pots . . . it is good for the hart and for the head. The seed cureth the infirmities of the hart, taketh away sorrowfulnesses which cometh of melancholie, and maketh a man merrie and glad.

Most country-bred people were familiar with herbs, and put them to use in various ways. There were several ways to prepare herbs for use, as follows:

Distillation. This method was used to extract essential oils, and was done by boiling herbs in a closed retort, open only at the top to let out the steam, which was then condensed in a tub of cold water, the oil or essence being dripped from the end of the tube leading from the retort.

Electuary. Herbs or roots were dried, then pounded to a powder. One ounce of powder to three

DR. FULLER AT WORK

Dr. Samuel Fuller prepares to lance a carbuncle as his patient sits uneasily on his stool. Mrs. Fuller acted as the doctor's nurse and also was midwife in the colony.

METHODS AND TOOLS FOR PREPARING HERBS

A. Absorption. A cloth was stretched over a wooden frame. On this cloth a liberal amount of melted fat was spread, and leaves or other parts of a plant were strewn over it. Placed in the sun over a grease pan, the fat absorbed the essence of the plant. The process was repeated with more herbs to increase the strength of the final product. This method was used to make pomades and ointments, which were stored in ceramic pots and covered with thin skin. *B.* Expression. A wooden screw-press was used to crush fruits and juicy plants, the liquid running off into a container. The juice was further processed in a variety of ways, if it was not to be drunk fresh. It could be made into an infusion or be distilled to make an extract. *C.* Maceration. This process used a double boiler, a pan set in a kettle filled with hot water. It was another way (besides absorption) of making ointments. Suet or other hard fat was put into the pan immersed in the hot water. Herbs with healing properties were then added to the suet. After a suitable length of time the boiling fat was decanted, strained, and put into pots. *D.* Distillation. A simple still was used to extract essential oils from plant parts or to make alcohol. It is not known if the Pilgrims made use of a still, but Dr. Fuller may have used one in the preparation of certain medicines.

On the stool in the foreground are bottles and salve jars *(E)*.

On the table in the foreground are a funnel *(F)*, pill roller set on a slab *(G)*, pill mass ready to be rolled *(H)*, mortar and pestle for crushing herbs *(I)*, and a mixing bowl *(J)*.

To the right of the table is a basketful of herbs *(K)*.

MAKING PILLS

The man is rolling out the pill mass. The woman is rolling a pill on her palm.

ounces of honey, mixed in a mortar with a pestle, was the proportion used in making an electuary.

Oils. Bruised herbs, flowers, or roots were placed in an earthen vessel and covered with oil. Left standing for two weeks, the herbs were then pressed to extract their goodness. Depending on their nature, these oils were used for rubbing, or for internal use (e. g., castor oil).

Juices. Fruits were placed in a linen bag which was put in a wooden screw-press to extract the juice. Succulent plants were pressed to extract their goodness.

Ointments. Herbs crushed in a mortar were mixed with hog grease or other fat. Kept in a warm place for several days, the fat was then boiled, strained, and poured into ceramic salve pots. These pots of Delftware had a lip around their top, over which parchment was stretched and tied with cord or leather cut from a thin-skinned animal.

Infusion. Hot water was poured over the particular part of the plant whose essence it was desired to extract. The infusion was allowed to cool before drinking.

Pills. Powdered herbs were mixed to a stiff paste

with honey, then rolled on a board. Pieces of the roll were pinched off and rolled between the palms of the hand, or between fingers for small pills.

Poultices. Chopped small, herbs were boiled down to a jelly, to which any suitable meal was added. If a firm poultice was required, suet was used to stiffen the mass. Poultices were usually applied as hot as the patient could bear them.

The merits accorded herbs may be gleaned from the quotes from an herbal in the following table:

Herb	Parts Used	Notes on Medical Use
angelica	root and seeds	"Comforts the heart, blood, and spirits."
honeywort	flowers and leaves	"For weak, watery, bleared eyes."
lemon balm	leaves	"Good for bites of venomous beasts; comforts the heart."
parsley	leaves, root, and seed	"For children when troubled with wind in the stomach."
sage	leaves	"Will retard the rapid progress of decay in the latter life."

Plant and animal extracts for medicinal use were classified as follows:

Classification	Medical Function	Sources
alteratives	to restore healthy bodily functions	sarsaparilla
anodynes	to allay pain	opium, belladonna
carminatives	to expel wind	asafetida, fennel, ginger, summer savory, parsley, and thyme
cathartics	to purge the body	jalap, bryony, castor oil
demulcents	to soothe mucous surfaces	acacia, slippery elm
diuretics	to increase urine flow	broom, wild carrot, foxglove, pine oil
ecbolics	to cause abortion	ergot
emollients	to soothe the skin	oils, lanolin and other animal fats
emetics	to induce vomiting	nux vomica (vomit nut)
hemostatics	to allay internal bleeding	ergot
motor-excitants	to increase muscular activity	nux vomica
refrigerants	to cool the body	dilute vegetable or mineral acids
sedatives	to induce sleep	opium, valerian, aconite
stimulants	to increase the activity of bodily functions	beer (2 percent alcohol), brandy, digitalis, oil of pine
tonics	to increase or restore physical or mental tone	gentian, hops, nux vomica
vermifuges	to expel worms	castor oil, scammony

The sad experience of the sickness, during which friends and relatives died, followed shortly afterwards by a period of near starvation, almost spelled doom for the new colony. However, the determination, courage, and fortitude of the Pilgrims pulled them through, and it was not long before others from England joined them, some to add to their trials, others to prove helpful in the growth of the colony.

Compared to the places where they had previously lived, New England was much healthier for the Pilgrims. It furnished abundant good water, rare in Europe, where streams or wells were apt to be contaminated with the wastes of factories or of humans. The air at Plymouth was fresh and pure, and the land abounded in game, fruits, nuts, and edible plants. True, it was some time before the colonists learned to live off the land, and at one time

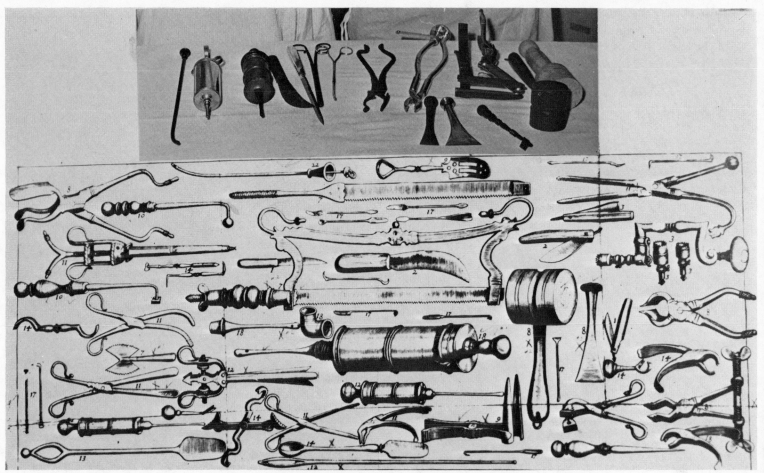

EARLY SURGICAL AND DENTAL INSTRUMENTS

Top: Reproductions of early surgical instruments contrasted with their modern counterparts. The reproductions are part of a medical exhibit at Plimoth Plantation, Plymouth, Massachusetts. Shown from left to right are urinary canula, syringe, periosteotome (surgical knife), urinary forceps, bone-holding clamp, bone chisel, bistoury (to right of chisel), dilating specula, and mallet.

Bottom: A wide selection of surgical instruments used in the seventeenth century. Several dental tools may be seen in the lower righthand corner.

they faced starvation due to this lack of knowledge; but then the Indians lived on a "feast or famine" basis, when game was scarce and fruits of the land were not available, as in winter. Thanks to the friendly Indians, a few of whom took to living in the colony, the necessary hunting and trapping skills were made known to the newcomers.

It is time now to see the part the Indians played in furthering the establishment of the colony on a sound basis. Bradford saw the hand of God in His sending to them not only a friendly Indian, but one who spoke enough of their language to make himself understood.

Chapter 8

Indian Benefactors

WHEN the Pilgrims first landed, of all the perils ashore none frightened them as much as the threat of an Indian massacre, such as had happened to the colonists at Jamestown. Undoubtedly there were wolves and bears lurking in the forest, but these they did not fear so much.

Having met Captain John Smith, one of the original Jamestown colonists, the Pilgrims were, no doubt, aware of his opinions concerning the Indians. Smith had described them this way: "Some are of disposition fearfull, some bold, some cauteous, all savage." It is also possible that the Pilgrims were familiar with other accounts of the Indians written by early explorers of the American continent. While some warned of the treachery and stealing habits of the Indians they encountered, others declared them childlike and trusting. It all depended on the approach used in contacting the Indians and how well the latter were treated. True, some Indians coveted the boats of the seamen, and there were instances of shallops and longboats being stolen, and of Indians being seen at sea in such boats, some of these, however, may well have been obtained in trade from the European fishermen who annually frequented the coast of New England and the Grand Bank off Newfoundland. It must be admitted that many of the European explorers gave the Indians ample provocation for stealing. To make some profit on a voyage most of them traded with the Indians, finding them easy marks; furs were traded for mere trinkets, but to balance the score the Indians stole whatever European goods they could lay their hands on. Retaliation was often harsh. Henry Hudson's men killed Indians for petty theft. Bartholomew Gosnold, who explored and named Martha's Vineyard in 1602, was one who discovered an Indian propensity for stealing. Following Gosnold a year later was Martin Pring, who wrote of giving "divers sorts of our meanest merchandise" in exchange for furs with the Indians. Pring had with him two great mastiff dogs with which he delighted in scaring the Indians. A disregard for the feeling of the natives, based no doubt on accounts of them picked up from returning seamen, seemed to be growing with each successive explorer. It was this ill treatment that resulted in deaths for unwary sailors caught ashore in Indian ambushes.

THE CAPTURE OF INDIANS BY EUROPEAN EXPLORERS

In 1611 Captain Edward Harlow sailed along Cape Cod, losing a longboat to Indians. In the scuffle to get it back he took captive four Indians, taking them back to England, where they were objects of curiosity but, on the whole, well treated. Such captures became a habit with other explorers and in 1614 Thomas Hunt, on a fishing and trading voyage, took five Indians of the Nauset tribe captive, sailing with them to Spain. There he attempted to sell them as slaves at twenty pounds per head. The Church intervened, taking in the Indians. One of these eventually found his way to England, where he learned the language. He somehow got back to America, probably on a fishing boat. This was Squanto, who was to be of great service to the Pilgrims when they landed at Plymouth in 1620.

One of the Indians captured by Harlow, Epenow, knowing the explorers' lust for gold, told a story of a gold mine in his island (Martha's Vineyard) and offered to take a party there to work it. Enough greedy men were found to back the venture, and a ship captained by one, Hobson, sailed and reached the island. There Epenow and his fellow Indians escaped to shore, leaving the ship's company no alternative but to return home empty-handed, not wishing to face the menacing Indians ashore. One Englishman was to die on this island, possibly to revenge the capture of Epenow and his fellow Indians. This man was Thomas Dermer, an old shipmate and fellow-venturer of Captain John Smith, who was fishing and fur trading off the New England coast in 1614. Dermer chose to live ashore on Newfoundland, and here he met Squanto. With him he made a journey in an open pinnace to Plymouth, where they found deserted Indian houses.

Not until they went inland did they find signs of life, and there Squanto introduced Dermer to a chief (probably Massasoit). After trading with the Indians Dermer and Squanto sailed back towards Newfoundland, the Indian wishing to be let off on the Maine coast, where he could be with other Indians. Later on, Dermer made a voyage as far as Jamestown, where he came down with fever. When recovered, he sailed up to Martha's Vineyard and there met his end. Some records state that he was betrayed by Epenow, but this was never proved. Certainly Dermer was the victim who paid for the mistreatment of Indians at the hands of previous visitors to that particular island.

THE INDIAN CACHE OF CORN THE PILGRIMS "BORROWED"

When circumstances forced Captain Christopher Jones to steer his ship on a course away from the Virginias, he rounded the tip of Cape Cod, coming to anchor in what is now Provincetown Harbor, whence exploring parties went in search of a colony site. Along the Cape they noted the presence of Indians, even finding a cache of their corn, which they "borrowed" with every intention of returning once their own harvest was in.

THE PILGRIMS' FEAR OF THE INDIANS

Upon landing at Plymouth, the Pilgrims saw no Indians. They were relieved by this, considering their weakened condition. During their time of sickness the Pilgrims even buried their dead by night in unmarked graves, lest the Indians discover their loss and wipe out those remaining. As they went about their task of cutting timber and erecting houses, they kept a sharp lookout for any signs of Indians. On occasion they saw smoke from Indian fires, but no Indians, until one day one of their number, concealed in the tall marsh grass, waiting to bag a duck, saw a file of Indians seemingly making their way towards the village site. He warned those working in the woods, who dropped their tools and ran back to the village to give warning. Nothing came of this encounter, except that the Indians made off with the tools left in the field. This incident caused the colonists to establish military orders, appointing Standish as their captain. He, in turn, organized the men into companies, and armed them. Thereafter, they took their arms with them whenever they left the village. The master of the *Mayflower* came ashore with some seamen, bringing part of the ordnance carried aboard ship, consisting of a minion (a 3-1/2-inch bore cannon), a saker (4-inch bore), and two bases (1-1/2-inch bore). These were set up on the hill above the village, where they commanded the sea and the surrounding country. It was also decided that a fort should be erected on top of the hill, with a palisade built from it to surround the village.

THE FIRST MEETINGS OF THE PILGRIMS AND THE INDIANS

Shortly after the establishment of military orders and the placing of ordnance, the long expected confrontation with Indians, or rather, one Indian, took place. It was not how the Pilgrims had imagined it might be, with hordes of savages, intent on killing, charging down upon them. It happened this way, and it must have seemed to the Pilgrims that the hand of Divine Providence was behind this event. One morning, a lone Indian marched boldly towards those gathered in the village, and welcomed them in English as he approached them. He said his name was Samoset, but he was not of those parts, having worked his way from Maine, where he had picked up some words of English from English traders and fishermen. Such a confrontation was disarming, to say the least; and the Pilgrims acted in a friendly manner towards this, the first Indian they had seen at close quarters.

It was from Samoset that the Pilgrims learned about the devastating plague that had wiped out most of the Indians of Plymouth. Samoset told them that he had joined the Indians under the sachem (chief) called Massasoit, who lived some fifteen miles from Plymouth. The Pilgrims, who had doubts about their planting a colony in the area, felt better, knowing that the tribe formerly occupying the site were dead. Wishing to show hospitality, the Pilgrims gave Samoset food to eat but, lacking beer, for which he asked, they gave him some "strong water" (brandy or gin). Their visitor seemed quite at home with the Englishmen and, in fact, was loath to leave as the day turned into night. Thinking it safer to put him aboard the *Mayflower* for the night, they made for the shallop, but the tide was low and the wind strong, making the trip too difficult; so they put him in the house of Stephen Hopkins and kept watch over him. Next day they sent him on his way with gifts of a knife, bracelet, and a ring, requesting him to return with skins to trade, and to please try to recover tools previously stolen by members of his tribe. This he promised to do.

It was Sunday when Samoset came again, bringing with him five other Indians who were dressed in deerskins, including trousers, rather than almost naked, as was Samoset on his first visit. All wore their hair shoulder length, cut across the forehead in a straight line. A few sported feathers in their hair, and one wore a foxtail dangling down his back. Bradford describes their being painted "in antic fashion" (like clowns), and their singing and dancing impressed him the same way. They paused to eat, mixing cornmeal they had brought with them with water to make a kind of porridge. When they wished to trade the skins they had brought, the Pilgrims told them it was not their way to trade on the Sabbath, but urged them to bring more furs on a future visit. The tools that had been stolen were duly returned, which pleased the Pilgrims, who now deemed the Indians honest. Five of the visitors took their leave, but Samoset pleaded sickness, and asked to be allowed to stay; his wish was granted, and he stayed until Wednesday. He then left, being presented with a hat, a pair of stockings, shoes, a shirt, and a piece of cloth to wear around his waist.

The Pilgrims' Welcome to Chief Massasoit

It was, say the records, a fair warm day on 22 March when the Indians returned, just as the Pilgrims were holding a meeting on public business. First came Samoset and Squanto, the latter more fluent in English than his companion; it was he who told the Pilgrims that their chief, Massasoit, was nearby, and wished one of their number to go to him. Edward Winslow was appointed to escort the chief into the Pilgrim village. As he drew near he saw that the chief had company; his brother,

Quadequina, and sixty braves. Squanto, who was with Winslow, had filled him in on names, and it was he who introduced Winslow to the assembled company. As was customary, the Pilgrim brought presents: a pair of knives and a copper chain with a jewel for the chief, and a knife and ear ornament for his brother. Some biscuits and butter were given to the two most important Indians, together with "strong water." In the manner of the English, Winslow made a fancy speech, transmitting words of peace from his king, saying the Pilgrims were his representatives in America; when the speech was concluded, Winslow invited the chief to accompany him to the Pilgrims' village. The chief's brother and his braves followed at some distance.

Governor Carver greeted them all, his words being translated for the chief by Squanto, although not too well, by all accounts. Food was produced, which the chief shared with his men. Hostages were exchanged, the chief not yet completely trusting the Englishmen. This is understandable, considering types like Hunt, who had made off with Indians from the nearby Cape Cod area. Carver and the chief sat down on a rug in a house then being erected, and more meat and drink was passed around. The Pilgrims were soon to discover the voracious appetites of the Indians, who ate whenever they could, and at other times had to fast when food was in short supply.

The Pilgrims' Mutual Assistance Pact with Massasoit

When the two principals got down to business, with Squanto acting as mouthpiece for the chief, it was agreed that all should live in peace, each defending the other if attacked. Carver said the Pilgrims would come to the chief's assistance if hostile Indians moved against him. In exchange, the chief was to warn hostile tribes not to move against the English. A sort of arms limitation agreement was made, prohibiting either party from bringing their arms into each other's camp. Carver emphasized the fact that King James was in back of the Pilgrims, though how the monarch could send help in time he did not say. There was kissing of hands, in the manner of such ceremonies, the chief feeling more at ease by then, and small wonder, since he

CONCLUSION OF PILGRIM-INDIAN PEACE PACT

William Bradford and the Great Sachem Massasoit shake hands after discussing a peace treaty between the Pilgrims and the Indians. Both sides, being apprehensive, have mounted a guard. Edward Winslow, who was to be liaison between the two parties, sits in the background.

had been plied with "strong water" throughout the proceedings. The Pilgrims seemed to feel that Massasoit was a man to be trusted, and they were not wrong, as was proved in time. Bradford describes him as being well-built, differing little in attire from his followers, except that he had a necklace of bone beads around his neck. His face was painted "a sad red, like murry [a brown dye], and oiled both head and face, that he looked greasily." His followers were painted "some black, some red, some yellow, some white, others with crosses and antic works." Some had skins across their shoulders; others were naked except for a leather apron around their loins. This was more the image of the savage the Pilgrims had imagined. Nevertheless, a peace had been made with the Indians, and they felt safer, at least for the present.

With hostages returned, the chief and his retinue departed, two most reluctantly; but the Pilgrims, seeing how they ate, did not want them hanging around eating up their none too abundant supplies. Massasoit had been very much taken with a sword, a breastplate, and a trumpet, which had been blown for him. He had wanted to trade for them, but this the Pilgrims refused to do, preferring to foist off trade truck of glittery beads and the like; this they continued to do when trading for beaver and other furs.

How the Pilgrims Regulated Visits from the Indians

That the recent visitors were fascinated by the white men was proved the next day, when a number of the Indians returned and asked for food. This was refused them, which puzzled them, inasmuch as they saw Samoset and Squanto behaving as if they belonged in the Pilgrim village. The colonists were happy to have these two Indians, who were wise in the ways of the wild, showing them how to live off the land.

However, when visits from other Indians became too frequent, the Pilgrims had to tell Massasoit to control them. They gave the chief a copper necklace which, they said, must be worn by any Indian coming on official business, in which case he would be fed. Others, without such a token, would be turned

SCENE FROM OCTOBER HARVEST FESTIVAL AT PLIMOTH PLANTATION

Indians and Pilgrims assemble around a fire, over which a sheep is being roasted. When they had it, the Pilgrims shared their food with their Indian friends.

away. This was a wise precaution, in view of the voracious appetites all the Indians seemed to have.

The Journey of Winslow and Hopkins to Massasoit's Camp

Feeling that Carver had done a good piece of work in arranging the peace treaty, the Pilgrims elected him to a second term as governor. He was, said Bradford, "a man well approved among us." Curious to find out how the other half lived, the Pilgrim leaders decided to send two of their number, Edward Winslow and Stephen Hopkins, to spy out the lay of the land and visit Massasoit in his own territory. Squanto went along as guide and interpreter. The party took along food for the journey, and the usual gifts, including the chain which was to be used on official visits by Indians coming to Plymouth. It was in June 1621 when this party set out on the trip, the distance being estimated by Squanto to be about fifteen miles. He proved to be no judge of distance, as mile after dreary mile was trudged. It was good weather, and the two Pilgrims liked what they saw of the country, with lots of fine timber along the way. They met Indians from time to time, most of whom were searching for nuts and fruits, which abounded in this virgin countryside. At one point, near day's end, they came upon Indians fishing, using a weir they had constructed for this purpose. Winslow and Hopkins were quick to trade for some fish for their supper. The Indians fishing were staying in the area, but had erected no shelter. As night came on, all lay down in the open and slept. Next morning the party from Plymouth got under way early, anxious to reach Massasoit's camp, which Squanto said was near the mouth of the river they had camped beside. The river was tidal, but the Pilgrims noted that at full tide their shallop would be able to navigate upstream. Six of the fishing Indians elected to walk along with the Plymouth party and, after about five miles of travel, the fishermen told the party to take off their trousers, as there was a ford to cross. At the crossing on the opposite shore were two Indians, standing in a menacing manner, their bows at the ready. However, signs that they came in peace put the two

at ease, and they bade the others join them. All then sat down to eat, and the two who had accosted them were given a share. Winslow gave them each a bracelet of beads. Lunch concluded, the party of nine got on their way, Squanto assuring them they were almost at their journey's end. They were hot and tired, but had quenched their thirst at the several springs along the way.

This time Squanto was right; they soon arrived at the camp of the chief but, wouldn't you know it, Massasoit was not there! Disappointed, they asked if he could be sent for, and were assured that he would be back before too long. Squanto, ever one to show off before fellow Indians, urged the Pilgrims to give a show of arms. This they commenced to do, but, seeing the fear on the faces of those assembled, gave up the idea. However, when Massasoit did appear, the two emissaries could not resist doing the chief honors, and gave him a volley of musket fire. Although this scared the wits out of the crowd, the chief seemed to consider it his due, taking it in good part. Then came the usual lengthy speeches, with the reason for their visit being spelled out, after which the chief was presented with a red linen horseman's coat and the chain, the use for which was then explained. Massasoit agreed to restrain his hungry braves, who must at this time have been suffering the pangs of hunger, for no food was offered the visitors, nor did there seem to be any around.

With official business at an end, the entertainment began, the Indians dancing their dances and singing their songs at the top of their lungs. Wearying at last, the chief retired to bed with his wife, beckoning the visitors to occupy the other end of his wigwam. There were no comforts, the bed being an elevated platform on which mats were piled for a mattress. Winslow described the experience this way: "Massasoit's men pressed by and upon us, so that we were worse weary of our lodging than of our journey." To add to their misery, the wigwam swarmed with lice and fleas, with the added nuisance of swarms of mosquitoes. Winslow and Hopkins were bitterly regretting their curiosity concerning the Indians' way of life.

The visitors had asked Massasoit to look out for any corn the Indians might want to trade and, anxious as the Pilgrims were to find out whose corn they had taken when exploring the Cape, they decided to head home by a route that would take them to this area. Wishing not to go back empty-handed, the Pilgrims challenged the Indians to target practice, bows and arrows against muskets, with furs as the prize for the best shooting, and trinkets if the Indians won. After seeing a demonstration of musket shooting with the use of scatter shot, which filled the target with holes, the Indians declined to compete. How any of them had strength enough for anything is surprising, no meals being served. Somebody procured two fish, which was but one bite apiece for the crowd of forty there assembled. The Pilgrims had to go on their way still hungry; they were anxious to be home for the Sabbath, wanting desperately to get deloused, take a bath, and fill their hungry bellies. They started on Friday before sunup. Massasoit urged them to stay and apologized for the lack of food and the rowdy behavior of his braves, who sang most of the night. Squanto was requested to stay behind to hunt for corn and furs, the chief delegating an Indian named Tokamahamon to be their guide. He proved to be good at his job, and useful in carrying the belongings of the two Englishmen, who felt the service was only their due. When the party arrived back at the fish weir, it was their luck to arrive when the fish were not running. They ate half a fish and a squirrel before turning in for the night. A few Indians who had tagged along with the party were sent on ahead to Nemasket on the Cape, home of the Nauset tribe, where all planned to meet next day. Those who stayed at the weir spent a miserable night, with rain, wind, and lightning to keep them from sleeping. There was no shelter, and all got soaking wet. Fortunately, a few fish were caught and roasted before the elements put out the fire. This was served for breakfast, prior to the journey to the Cape, which was made in pouring rain. What luck they had in procuring corn is not reported; just the fact that the travelers reached Plymouth wet, exhausted, and very hungry. It had been a revealing trip, but did nothing to raise the Pilgrims' opinion of the Indian, who remained in their eyes an ignorant savage with few redeeming features except his apparent friendliness.

Despite the Pilgrims' low opinion of the Indians, they did not hesitate to adopt Indian methods of living off the land. Much of what the Pilgrims learned from the natives proved essential to the survival of the Plymouth colony.

THE INDIAN WAY OF LIFE

The following discussion of seventeenth-century Indian life relies upon accounts written by early visitors to New England which describe the Indians' dwellings, agriculture, hunting methods, and general way of life.

Indian Dwellings

Indian houses were called wigwams. They were made by setting poles in the ground around the plan, which, in longhouses, was rectangular in shape. A smaller version, used in summer camps, was built like half a sphere. The bent-over poles were tied together with natural vines or strong grasses, to form a rounded roof. A door was set in each end, and a smoke-hole was left in the central part of the roof. The wigwams were covered with bark, for winter use, and with grass mats in summer. Around the sides in the longhouse a platform was built, about two feet off the ground, made from poles lashed together. On top of this mats were piled to make a sleeping place. Warmth was provided by a fire built within a circle of stones at the center of the wigwam. Over this was a structure to hold a cooking pot. Weapons and skins for clothing were hung on antlers fixed to the walls. The Indians lived, ate, and slept in the wigwams during the winter months. In summer they lived outdoors, going inside their domed shelters in inclement weather. On hunting trips they slept under the sky, or under trees if it rained. All were hardy, requiring little clothing, as was indicated when Samoset first called on the Pilgrims naked except for a leather apron at his loins—and this was in the dead of winter. Winter wigwams were made large, as Champlain indicated on his map of Plymouth Harbor (not then so named). Summer dwellings were much smaller, intended only as shelters while hunting. Frames were left in place, the mats only being taken away when camp was abandoned.

SUMMER TYPE OF INDIAN WIGWAM

The frame of bent branches was left up when camp was broken, the woven mats used as cover being taken away. Mats were woven from bark strips or suitable grasses. A mat being woven is shown hanging from the tree at right.

Indian Agriculture

The cultivation of land by the Indians was most primitive; yet it was the means of providing them with staple foods, corn (maize) being the principal crop. Living as they did in virgin forest land, the cultivation of the soil presented problems. To clear enough ground for crops required destroying some of the forest, which meant very little to them, except as a game preserve. Since the Indians had no axes,

their method of clearing ground was the burning down of acres of trees. To burn down a tree the Indians had to keep a fire burning day and night; this burned away the base so that the top-heavy branches would topple it.

The Indians, although they did not know it, were benefiting the forests when they fired the undergrowth to clear trails for themselves, making for swifter passage when chasing game. Cleared of undergrowth, the trees grew better, and were little damaged by fire, which quickly flashed through them.

The wood ash of the burned trees would act as a fertilizer to some degree, but the Indians, at least those at Plymouth, made use of fish (alewives) for fertilizer, setting three fish, amidst which they put several kernels of corn, in each scooped hole. Over all they made a mound of earth. They planted peas and pumpkins between rows, to shade the early shoots, and to provide other food. When the seeds of wheat and barley the Pilgrims planted failed to germinate, they adopted the Indian method of corn planting. The Pilgrims did not bring a plow with them from England, which is just as well, the ground of Plymouth being stony.

When the Pilgrims' first harvest came at last, sometime in October 1621, they decided to hold a harvest thanksgiving, which was the custom in England. Now was the time to invite some of their Indian friends to share in their bounty, as a gesture of thanks for their help. Their Indian guests came bearing five deer as their contribution to the feast, a rare treat of fresh venison. After blessing the food and thanking God for his bountiful harvest, all tucked into the meal, filling their long-denied stomachs with wholesome and tasty food, a welcome change from smoked fish. After their food had settled, games were played, the Indians danced and sang, and there were competitions in shooting, the Indians with their arrows, the colonists firing off their muskets. It was a happy time, an interlude between one fast and another one to come, although none suspected this at the time.

Ever mindful of recurring food shortages, the Indians grew as much corn as they could manage to care for, eating the pounded kernels in a gruel, or making it into cakes which they baked on hot stones. Care was taken to keep seed for the following year. This was put into grass sacks or baskets, and buried under a mound of earth. It was such a cache the Pilgrims found when exploring Cape Cod.

The Indians discovered that land too often used for a crop did not yield plentifully, so they let land lie fallow for a year or two before replanting. They did not seem to mind having a garden plot several miles away from their habitation. Each family

raised its own crops. Spring planting was done when the leaves of the white oak were as big as a mouse's ear. In a good season there could be two crops of corn.

The Indians had few garden tools. Early travelers wrote that the Indians used tools made of wood, bone, and shell, the latter being fixed on the end of a pole, to roughly resemble a hoe. Grubbing for roots was done with a pointed stick. It is no wonder, then, that the Indians coveted the white man's tools, and made off with them whenever the opportunity to do so presented itself. This, as we have already seen, happened to the Pilgrims, who were lucky to get their tools back.

Indian Hunting and Trapping Methods

All able-bodied Indians were initiated at an early age into the techniques of hunting, which was done with bow and arrow, by trapping and snaring, and with the bare hands. Fleet of foot, and wise in the ways of animals, the Indians could bag a deer with ease. The Indians furnished much of the venison the Pilgrims ate, since shooting with an arrow was quicker than loading and firing a musket. Moreover, Indians were skilled stalkers, creeping up on their prey with little noise, something a colonist in heavy shoes and with no skill at walking lightly could not do.

A safe and sure method of bagging a deer was to fell a tree on a known deer trail. The deer, being browsers, would move in to eat the foliage. Hidden among the leaves was a noose, tied to a sapling, which was bent over and lightly secured. A deer getting its head in the noose would, when trying to extricate itself, trip the held-down sapling, which would spring back upright, tightening the noose to choke the deer. Waiting Indians would cut the animal down, skin it, and cut it into convenient-sized pieces for transportation back to camp. In a treeless place, the Indians would dig a pit across a deer trail, covering it with light poles over which foliage was placed. An unwary animal passing over the trail would fall into the pit, from which escape was almost impossible. The animal would be stunned and killed, and hauled back to camp, sometimes on a pole slung between two men.

Besides deer, larger game included bear, elk, and

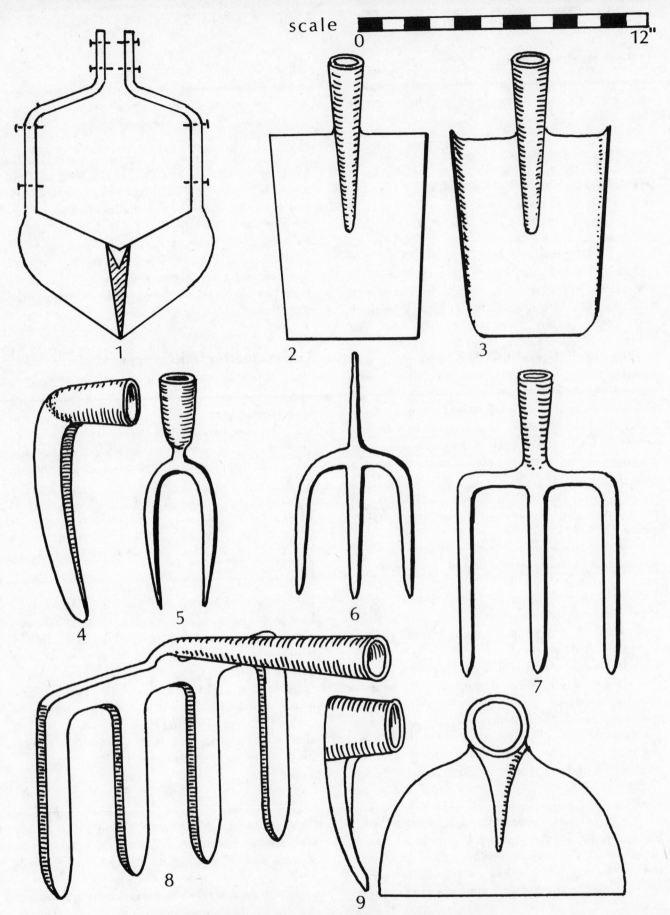

scale
0   12"

SEVENTEENTH-CENTURY FARM AND GARDEN TOOLS

1. Iron shodding for a wooden spade. The shaded portion is the slot into which the bottom of the blade was fitted. The shodding was secured to the wood with nails. *2.* Blacksmith-made iron spade with a socket for the handle. *3.* Blacksmith-made iron shovel with a socket for the handle. *4.* Iron pick for breaking hard ground. *5.* Iron pitchfork with socket for wooden handle. *6.* Small iron garden fork with tang, which was driven into the end of a wooden handle. *7.* Larger garden fork with socket for handle. *8.* Muck fork for cleaning out animal shelters. A long wooden handle was fitted into the socket. *9.* Front and side views of one type of hoe. The size of a hoe was determined by the job it had to perform, whether it were weeding or breaking up ground. Lacking plows until 1632, the Pilgrims used hoes for a variety of purposes.

ENGLISH TOOLS EXCAVATED AT JAMESTOWN

Left: **Billhooks.** *Right:* **Hoes. These tools were typical of the period, and similar ones may have been used by the Plymouth colonists of 1620.**

moose, which the Indians shot with arrows or trapped in various ways. Unafraid of bears, they would drive them into their camp, and there slay them, thus obviating the need to lug back a heavy carcass from a distance.

By shooting a massed flight of arrows into a flock of geese or ducks, Indian hunters were able to bag quite a number of birds. Fleet-footed Indians were said to be able to run down rabbits and scoop them up on the run. They also could grab a rodent as it emerged from its hole in the ground. The Indians even caught rats, which were plentiful in the marshes, providing both food and fur; muskrat fur

was valued almost as much as beaver by some traders.

Indian Fishing Methods

The Indians were also adept at securing seafood, and they passed their fishing skills along to the Pilgrims. Fish were caught in weirs, eels in traps, and lobsters by hand. The weirs were cunningly made by driving stakes into the mud, arranged wide at the mouth and tapering to a narrow opening farther upstream. The fish swam into the enclosure in schools, but, after passing through the narrow

FIRING A MUSKET

This page from a Dutch military manual illustrating the step-by-step procedure for loading and firing a musket demonstrates that the musket was an unsuitable gun for hunting, if more than one shot was required to down an animal.

TRAPS AND SNARES

A. Fox trap, used before hunting with horse and hounds. This drawing was suggested by an illustration in *A Booke of Fishing with Hooke and Line* (1590) by Leonard Mascall. Mascall also mentions the use of iron traps, as does Markham, a seventeenth-century writer, in a book on trapping. *B.* Fishing and trapping. This drawing is also based on a picture in Mascall's book. *C.* Pitfall, with baited stick. Any animal venturing out on the limb topples into the deep pit and cannot get out. *D.* Choking snare, set in a known animal track. A running animal would be brought up short as the cord tied to the cross-stick ran out, and the noose would choke it to death. *E.* Deadfall. Any bird or animal attempting to get the bait would release the catch set in a notch in the tree trunk, thus allowing the heavy rock to fall and crush it. *F.* Snare nets. This drawing is based on one of a set of prints entitled "Rabbit Hunting without Guns" by Francis Barlow (1671). The prints may be found in the Folger Library.

17th century Fishermen   ◄ from old prints ►   16th century Eel catcher   eel spear

Fish weir   Smoke-drying fish

FISHING

Top left: Seventeenth-century fishermen hauling in their net. *Top right:* Sixteenth-century eel catcher. The eel trap in his boat suggests the fisherman was after eels, but he may also have been fishing for bait with his dip-net. *Top far right:* Eel spear, unchanged in form to this day. The barbed tines held the slippery eels until the fisherman could extract them.

Bottom left: Fish weir. This one, in the tidal estuary of a stream, was designed to catch fish as they swam upstream. The fish found themselves trapped in the corral, whence they were hauled ashore with hand nets. The narrow mouth of the corral could be sealed off to prevent the fish from escaping. *Bottom right:* Smoke-drying fish. The fish were slit and gutted, then hung on poles in a smoky fire to dry and cure. Such fish were eaten when the weather was too rough for fishing, as in the winter months. Fires for smoking fish were built with alternate wet and dry wood, the dry to burn readily, the wet to make smoke. Hardwoods were preferred for this purpose, their ashes being saved to make lye, used in soapmaking.

opening, became confused and were not all able to escape. In the pond above the narrow opening, the Indians clubbed or speared the fish, which they then threw ashore. Often the Indians relied upon simpler means to catch fish. Squanto showed the Pilgrims how easy it was to tread eels out of the river mud and catch them with bare hands. He also taught the colonists how to catch alewives. Just

after the *Mayflower* departed in April 1621, the brook near the village was literally teeming with these fish, swimming upstream to their spawning grounds in the ponds above Plymouth. Armed with baskets, the colonists scooped load after load of fish from the stream, piling them up along the banks. Fresh fish was a welcome change from the salt beef they had brought with them from England and all ate their fill, but Squanto told them some should be saved for when the flow ceased. He showed them how to dry and smoke the fish to preserve them, building racks over fires outdoors.

The Feast-and-Famine Existence of the Indians

From the foregoing it can be seen that the Indians were fully capable of obtaining food when it was plentiful; but when snow was on the ground and the game birds flew south, it became more difficult to feed a tribe of several hundred people, not all of whom were hunters. That is why the Indians made every effort to smoke and dry meat and fish for winter food, and stored their corn, using it more sparingly during the winter. Despite these efforts, they led a feast-or-famine existence. When food was plentiful, they ate all they could stuff down; in the winter they lived from hand to mouth, on the verge of starvation at times.

Gorging the stomach in times of plenty gave rise to physical ills, particularly of the digestive system, chronic constipation being one of them. Winslow was summoned by chief Massasoit's braves when their own medicine man failed to cure their leader. On reaching the chief's bedside, Winslow diagnosed his trouble right away, after being told of a feast held a few days earlier. A purge was administered, which eased the chief's bellyache, so that he was soon crying for food. Winslow wisely fed him only a soup made from fowl.

INDIANS BUILDING A FISH WEIR

Indian Medicine

There is very little literature on the subject of medicine among the woodland tribes of New England, and we know little of their contact with other tribes, from which they might have learned of herbs and plants used for medicines. It is quite likely the Indians knew of and used wintergreen for colds. Most known Indian remedies were strong-tasting, usually bitter or sour. They made use of roots of plants, one of which was said to taste like ginger. Senega may have been one of their remedies for bronchitis. They are said to have chewed the resin that exudes from balsams, and they stuffed pillows with the fragrant needles, on the theory that the scent cleared the head. It is quite likely that the Indians near Plymouth learned something about herbs and their uses from the Pilgrims, most of whom were old hands at family medicine. In turn, the colonists may well have learned a few new tricks about native plants from the Indians. The herbs included in the accompanying list are those known to have been used by Indians in other parts of America, and were reported on by travelers in their territory. In addition to the listed herbs, In-

MEDICINAL PLANTS USED BY AMERICAN INDIANS

Plant	Medical Use
American mountain ash	The inner bark was placed over wounds to aid in healing. The red berries, containing ascorbic acid, were used as a remedy for scurvy.
Buttercup	An infusion of the pulverized roots was used to wash wounds. According to Gerard's herbal, the Indians placed the bruised leaves over ulcers to cure them.
Sweet gum	The resin which exudes from the bark was placed over wounds to draw out the pus.
White oak	The bark yields tannin, an astringent used by Indians as a cure for diarrhea.
Skunk cabbage	The root was boiled in water, and the liquid drunk to aid in coughing up phlegm.
Mullein, Indian tobacco, and Jimsonweed	The dried roots and leaves were smoked to relieve head congestion.
Arnica, gentian, and horsemint	These were used for strains and bruises.
Sunflower and yellow dock	The leaves were crushed to release their juices and used as remedies for blisters and boils.
Wild pansy, blue flax, corn, and pine trees	These were used in the treatment of boils and swellings. Corn was used as a poultice, and pine gum was mixed with fat.
Scarlet mallow, horsetail fern, and yarrow	These were used to treat burns.
Balm of Gilead (poplar family)	The resinous material covering the buds was mixed with fat to make an ointment which was placed up the nose to ease breathing.
Wintergreen, or checkerberry	This was used as a tea to relieve colds. The leaves were rubbed on swollen joints to ease the pain of rheumatism.
Catnip	A tea made from the leaves was drunk to relieve colic.
White pine, wild cherry, and sarsaparilla	These were cold remedies.
Blackberry, red cedar, and sweet fern	These provided remedies for diarrhea.
Bayberry, dogwood, willow, and fever root	These were used to induce sweating in the treatment of fevers.
Trumpet honeysuckle	The leaves were chewed and laid over insect bites, and onion and garlic buds were rubbed on them to relieve itching.

dians of the Southwest and Mexico used a number of plants having narcotic properties, some of which are used today by doctors, but not in their original state.

Although the Indians knew nothing about the medical theories of Paracelsus, they did live an outdoor life, with plenty of fresh air, things the Renaissance doctor advocated as being conducive to good health. The Indians put great faith in their sweat lodge. This was a small wigwam in which they sat, surrounded with hot stones, over which they threw water to raise steam. They believed this process sweated out evil, and relieved aches and pains. The sweat lodge has its modern-day counterpart in the Turkish bath and the sauna, except that the latter uses dry heat, not steam, to achieve its purpose.

Whether the Indians considered tobacco a medicine or a pleasure we do not know; yet when it was first introduced into England, the doctors seized on it as a head-clearer, advising a patient to blow smoke through his nostrils. Harsh as tobacco was in the days before the weed was processed to achieve mildness, the doctors may have hit upon a remedy which would, at least, make the eyes water and the nose sting.

Women's Work Among the Indians

There was a well-defined division of labor between Indian men and women. The work of cultivation fell to the women. It was also the women who scoured the woods for fruits and nuts in season, and for medicinal plants and flavoring herbs. Girls accompanied their mothers, and so learned at an early age to recognize the plants. Indian women sewed together the skins of animals killed by the Indian men to make blankets and garments. A bearskin was prized as a bed cover by the Indians. For their dress they preferred deerskin, which they wore over their shoulder. Some Indians wore what the Pilgrims described as "Irish" pants on their legs; these were made from the skin of a deer.

Men's Work Among the Indians

Indian men spent much of their time hunting,

fishing, and making canoes. Dugout canoes were a byproduct of the Indian method of clearing land to make room for crops. A burned-down tree was quite often made into a dugout canoe. The Indians used fire to hollow it out and to shape its ends. Burning was controlled by the use of wet clay set around the edge. Burned wood was chipped out with a sharp-edged shell. A large birch tree was stripped of its bark when a bark canoe was to be built*. The bark was soaked to make it pliable, then bent to shape, being sewn together with leather thongs or strong vines. Strengthening wood ribs were bent and set in place, with several crossbraces being set in from thwart to thwart.

PILGRIM RELATIONS WITH THE INDIANS

When not actively engaged in one of their traditional tasks, Indian men idled around their village, and this idleness, said visiting Europeans, gave rise to stealing, lying, and worse, bearing out the old saying that the devil finds work for idle hands. Although many of their fellow Europeans regarded the Indians as untrustworthy, the Pilgrims' relations with the tribes of Massachusetts were generally harmonious. Word that the Pilgrims were fair in their dealings with the Indians spread to tribes other than that of Massasoit, as was proved when Winslow and Hopkins paid their visit to the Nausets' village. While the two Pilgrims were there, an old woman cried out against these white men, her three sons having been captured by Hunt and sold into slavery in Spain. She was calmed down, given gifts, and made to know that these were not like Hunt, but good men. It was discovered that it was from the Nausets that corn had been borrowed by the Pilgrims, and this was replaced when the colonists' harvest was in. Such good conduct could not have failed to convince the Indians that these were, indeed, good people who lived at Plymouth.

---

*Not used by the Indians of Plymouth, but by tribes living farther north (Canada).

INDIAN AGRICULTURE

Crops were planted and tended by the women, while the men were busy hunting for food. Lacking felling axes, the Indians burned down trees to make room for planting crops, setting their seed between the burned stumps.

How the Pilgrims Dealt with Hostile Indians

Although the Nausets were friendly enough, the Narragansetts felt ill-disposed towards the Pilgrims and Massasoit, who had allied himself with them. The Pilgrims learned of this when Winslow was sent to Massasoit, who was reported to be ill. We have previously recounted this visit, during which the chief was nursed back to health. Massasoit warned Winslow that the molesting of Indian women by the men of Thomas Weston (see chapter 10) was making the Narragansetts angry, and they were planning to raid Weston's newly set up colony at Wessagusset. Winslow was also told that the Massachusetts Indians were spoiling for a raid on Plymouth, to get rid of all the white men in their territory. Despite the fact that they despised Weston's men, the colony leaders could hardly let them perish at the hands of Indians who, once they got the blood lust, might well turn on the Plymouth colonists, as was the fate at Jamestown. Standish, who took an armed party to aid the Englishmen, was forced to kill the Indian ringleaders, after which some of Weston's men abandoned their new colony and sailed for Maine, while others returned to Plymouth with Standish.

Standish reacted equally decisively when the Narragansetts raided Massasoit's village, capturing him, some of his braves, and Squanto, who was there at the time. Hobomok brought word to the Pilgrims concerning this raid, saying also that he thought Squanto had been slain. He said that Corbitant, a petty sachem of the Pocasset tribe, but under Massasoit, had stirred up the trouble, and it was he with whom they should deal. Hobomok had recently come to live with the Pilgrims, and was in the service of Standish, who recognized his merits and his fine physique. Standish assembled his guard and, with Hobomok as guide, went to look for Corbitant and, if Squanto was not dead, rescue him and Massasoit. In so doing he was keeping the Pilgrims' obligation under the peace treaty to offer aid in time of trouble. Losing their way, the party spent a wet, miserable night, but next day came to a wigwam full of Indians. The latter put up a brief fight, and some Indians were hurt, but they told where Corbitant might be found, also that Squanto was not dead. Standish's men recovered both Massasoit and Squanto, but Corbitant escaped.

INDIAN MAID PREPARING BARK FOR WEAVING

Such bark was used for weaving mats similar to the one on which the Indian girl is sitting. The inner and outer bark of some trees was used for this purpose.

The injured were taken back to Plymouth for treatment by the doctor.

This incident prompted the Pilgrims to send a party north to seek out the Massachusetts tribe, which, they had heard from Massasoit, had issued threats against the Pilgrims. This tribe lived on and around the bay on the site now occupied by Boston. Going in the shallop, they were able to explore the bay, finding there many islands, some of which showed signs of occupancy, but no visible Indians. Even ashore this held true: lots of houses, but no Indians. There was evidence that the Indians had not long been gone from there; lobsters were piled up along the beach, and an Indian woman with a basket was the sole occupant of that area. She told where the tribe was hiding, and Standish and his men went to seek them out. They met the chief, who said that the Abnakis were harassing them, keeping them on the run. Standish assured the chief that he would see that they were not harmed, giving him the "King James as protector" speech, such as was delivered to Massasoit. Just what help the English crown could offer and when it might come he did not say, but the chief seemed relieved. Standish saw evidence that the Indians were afraid in the shape of a fort they had built, circular in form, with high, pointed poles set in the ground, and with a moat on each side of them. The chief took Standish and his party to the rest of the Indians, where there was a meal of boiled cod awaiting them. After the meal they did some trading, during which Squanto told the Pilgrims to strip the women of their furs, his excuse being that they had been unfriendly and thus deserved no consideration. Although Standish refused to do this, the women took off their furs, leaving them naked but modest. This trip seemed to reassure Standish that the Pilgrims had little to fear from these Indians, whose number had been greatly reduced by the same epidemic that had killed off the Indians at Plymouth. All this was duly recorded in letters sent back to England on the next ship.

Standish, a man of direct action, had proved to himself and to the surrounding Indians that he was not a man to be trifled with. When he had received the first Indian challenge, in the form of a bundle of arrows wrapped in a snakeskin, which Squanto said meant trouble, Standish returned the skin, replacing the arrows with lead musket balls.

Squanto saw to it that the challengers did not mistake this for anything but a counterchallenge. They got the message, and went away. They knew they had little chance against bullets, and they were much afraid of the loud explosions of the Pilgrim muskets. The word must have got around, and no further challenges were issued by any of the surrounding tribes.

THE DEATH OF SQUANTO

Shortly after harvest in 1622 the Pilgrims lost their faithful friend and interpreter, Squanto. It happened during a trip in search of additional corn, which the Indians were sometimes willing to trade. Bradford was in charge of the shallop, Standish being sick at the time, and Squanto went along as guide and contact man. In a harbor on Cape Cod, the Indian came down with a fever and bled profusely from the nose. Before two days had passed he was dead, begging with his last breath that Bradford ask his God to accept him into the white man's heaven. No doubt Bradford reassured Squanto that God would grant his wish. This was a touching end to the Indian who had been so helpful to the newly arrived colonists.

Despite the valuable services which he had rendered to the Pilgrims, Squanto had, at times, caused trouble in the camps of the Indians and Pilgrims alike, telling Massasoit one thing and the opposite to the Pilgrims. Why he did this is not clear, but he was jealous of Samoset and Hobomok, the other two Indians who lived with the Pilgrims, and perhaps was trying to show he was superior to them. At any rate Squanto informed the Pilgrims that Massasoit was tired of keeping peace and planned to raid the village. When confronted, the chief denied this and, hearing the rumor originated with Squanto, asked that he be turned over to him for punishment. The Pilgrims were loath to lose their useful Indian, and so delayed in sending him away. Fortunately, Massasoit's anger soon cooled, and Squanto was saved, which was a relief for all concerned.

INDIANS WHO LIVED WITH
THE PILGRIMS

Samoset continued to live with the Pilgrims, and

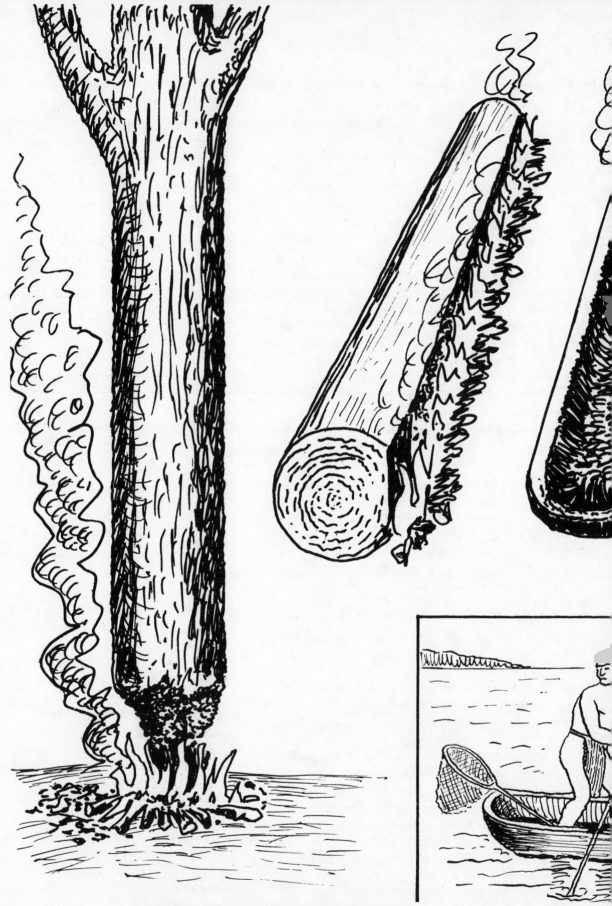

MAKING AND USING A DUGOUT CANOE

Left: The first step in making a dugout canoe was to burn down a tree by lighting a fire at its base and waiting for the weakened trunk to topple. *Center:* A flat face was burned along the felled log; then the trunk was hollowed out by fire along its length. The burning was controlled by the placing of wet clay as the fire burned down into the log. *Right:* The charred wood was scooped out with large clam shells, which served as both scoops and chisels. A fire was built at each end to round the canoe. *Bottom right:* The Indians used dugout canoes for fishing offshore. Early explorers admired the way the Indians handled their canoes, even in heavy surf. This type of dugout canoe was used by the Indians of Cape Cod and Plymouth.

DEBARKING A TREE

An Indian peeling off long strips of bark from a tree, with which to weave mats and baskets.

is reported to have died around 1653. Hobomok lived in Standish's house for years, even when the latter moved to a farm he established in Duxbury. The Indian chief Massasoit lived until 1661, having kept the promise he made to remain at peace with the Pilgrims. This peace lasted for over fifty years, coming to an end at the start of King Philip's War in 1675. The Pilgrims had proved that the Indians, if treated well, would give no trouble. In contrast, the colonists at Jamestown, who had no use for the Indians, suffered several attacks.

With the death of their fierce chief, the Indians retired onto their own preserves, later becoming wards of the colony. At Plymouth, the Pilgrims kept their word to Massasoit, who learned to like and respect them. Friendly relations with the Indians were a boon to the colony, for without the help of the Indians it is doubtful if the Pilgrims could have survived those first hard years at Plymouth.

Chapter 9

Commerce and Industry of the Pilgrims

FROM the very first, the London backers of the Plymouth colony expected it to pay a return on their investment. Not only did they have little understanding of the hardships faced by the Pilgrims in the New World but they added to the troubles of the colonists by sending to America boatload after boatload of new settlers without tools or adequate supplies. (Most of the boats sent by the London Adventurers were only half the size of the *Mayflower* and had little cargo space.) Shortly after the Pilgrims' first Thanksgiving feast a ship, which caused some alarm until the English flag was seen flying from the mainmast, sailed into Plymouth Harbor. The ship was the *Fortune*, sent out by the London Adventurers with colonists as reinforcements. Theirs had been a trip even longer than that of the *Mayflower*, and their food was almost exhausted. Those who came had only the clothes upon their backs.

Things were not all bad, for among the passengers were known faces of dear friends.

Robert Cushman, who had arranged Pilgrim affairs in England, came ashore with his son. With him he brought a patent which, in essence, approved the Mayflower Compact, and gave assurance that after seven years the colony would be given definite boundaries, and every settler 100 acres of land. Elder Brewster was glad to welcome his son Jonathan, and two men who were to have a great future in America, Thomas Prence, a future governor, and Philip de la Noye, ancestor of Franklin D. Roosevelt. Of the rest who came ashore Bradford said "some of them (were) wild enough."

Cushman told the Pilgrim leaders that their backers were much annoyed that the *Mayflower* had returned empty of cargo, and he urged them to load up the *Fortune* with whatever they could to go towards paying off their debt. All hands turned to loading the *Fortune* with clapboards and two hogsheads of furs, all they had; but Cushman, who returned on the ship, promised to explain the plight of the colonists to their backers, and the reasons why cargoes had to be skimpy for a time. Sad to relate, the *Fortune's* cargo never reached England, being pirated off the French coast; Cushman was allowed to proceed to England, where he had a sad tale to tell. Thus did the first attempt to pay off the debts of the Pilgrims fail.

Early in the year 1622 a shallop appeared in the bay, and proved to contain some of Thomas Weston's men from the fishing fleet off Maine. They came with a message which asked the Pilgrims to provide them with corn, as they were planning to establish a colony. The Pilgrims were not able to supply their needs, nor could they feed and entertain them as Weston had requested. All they represented to the colonists were seven more mouths to feed, which meant less for everyone else.

Other troubles surfaced as two more Weston ships came into harbor. These were the *Charity* and *Swan*, which landed at the end of June 1622, putting ashore "sixty lusty men." They brought the bad news about the fate of the *Fortune,* together with a letter from one of the London Adventurers in which was a warning that Weston was aiming to get all the profits from New England into his own hands. Again there was no food, and little else put ashore from the ships. Although harvest time was near, it had not yet come, which made the situation desperate. A ray of hope came with the arrival of the *Bona Nova* from the fishing grounds off Maine. The captain revealed that food might be obtained from Weston's boats in Maine; so Bradford sent Winslow and a crew in the shallop to find the ships. This he did by following the *Bona Nova* back to the island of Monhegan. There he found over thirty ships, from which he obtained a good supply of food, enough to eke out the Pilgrims' supplies until harvest.

With Winslow's return there was more food for everyone, but not yet full rations. All looked forward to harvest, but Weston's men could not wait until then. Before the corn was ripe they stole ears of it under the cover of darkness. Greedy, and ill-disciplined, none had done any work in the colony; yet they were eating food that was intended for the colonists, and on which they would have to live until the following year. Not content with stealing

the Pilgrims' corn, they had allied themselves to the Indians, performing all manner of menial tasks in order to eat and carouse, much to the disgust of those they served. Weston's men were the product of city slums in England, and went to sea to escape the authorities, and to keep out of jail. The colonists were glad to see the backs of Weston's troublesome men, who departed in the fall of 1622 to Wessagusset (now Weymouth) to set up a colony of their own.

TRADE WITH THE INDIANS: EXCHANGING TRINKETS FOR FURS AND CORN

Shortly before harvest, the ship *Discovery,* on her way to England from Jamestown, called in at Plymouth. The Pilgrims went aboard and traded with the captain to obtain trinkets which they intended to exchange with the Indians for furs and corn. They had to pay a good price for truck, but were glad to get it. Aboard the ship was John Pory, to whom we are indebted for one of the few accounts of the Pilgrims written by outsiders. Pory gave the Pilgrims high marks for what they had accomplished, particularly in the way of defenses. He was grateful for the hospitality shown him while in Plymouth, and for books lent him to read on the voyage home.

Bradford made haste to turn the trinkets to good purpose by trading them for corn from the Nauset Indians on Cape Cod. This was the voyage during which Squanto died. The corn and beans procured were not of immediate use to the colonists, being left on the cape, along with the shallop, when a storm drove the party ashore, where they were forced to bury them and hike back home overland. With their harvest in, the Pilgrims were content to let their Cape Cod cache stay buried until the following February, when Standish retrieved it, and sailed it back in the shallop to Plymouth.

By 1623 the colonists were becoming better at living off the land and sea, learning when certain fish came into the harbor, and digging for ground nuts when nothing else was available. They trapped what game they could with Indian methods. Lobsters were always in good supply, and the shores were full of shellfish. Nevertheless, the

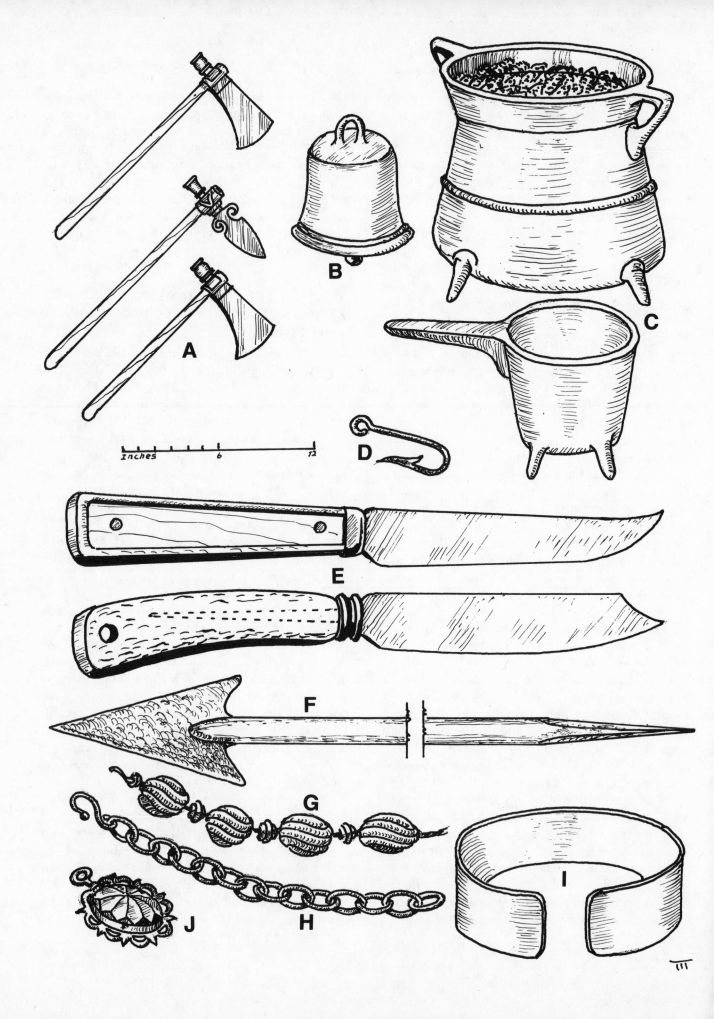

Inches 6 12

A B C D E F G H I J

colonists were not yet free from trouble. They suffered a severe drought at the time their crops were maturing, and had it not been for providential rains near harvest time, they may well have had no crops at all. As it was, they saved a good part of this 1623 crop, giving thanks to God for sending the rain.

Shortly after Thanksgiving in 1623 two ships sailed into harbor a week apart. The first was the *Anne,* the second the *Little James,* bringing a total of sixty new colonists, some of whom were old friends from Leyden, or relatives left behind when the *Mayflower* sailed. The new arrivals were dismayed when they regarded their old friends, who were clad in ragged clothing which hung like bags from their scrawny figures. The fresh reinforcements must have wondered what they had let themselves in for. Even though there were more mouths than ever to feed, however, they all managed to survive. The colonists dug for ground nuts to eke out their diet, and lived off the land as far as possible. Having learned how to dry and smoke fish and game, they did not have to pull in their belts in quite the same degree as the previous winter. Things were looking up. When Winslow, who had sailed on the *Anne,* laden with a cargo of clapboards and beaver skins, returned the following March, he was wise enough to bring three cows and a bull back with him, as well as additional supplies and clothing.

TRADE WITH THE INDIANS: EXCHANGING CORN FOR HIDES

From 1624 on, the Pilgrims suffered no longer from hunger. By 1625 there was enough corn grown at Plymouth to trade it in Maine, and with a skilled boat-builder among them now, they had more boats to travel in. This man had arrived on the *Charity,* and he soon had two more shallops built, there being no lack of timber for such a purpose. One of these was rigged with a half-deck under which the cargo could be stowed to protect it from breaking seas. In this boat Winslow took corn to Maine and traded it for 400 pounds of beaver and other skins.

THE ATTAINMENT OF PROSPERITY

Overland travel was made easier after 1625, since several horses had been shipped in. However, it was often quicker to make a journey by sea than by land, there being no roads, only trails through woodland. The cows had calved by this time and were thriving on the lush grass along the riverbanks and in the meadows. Pigs were there also; these could find plenty of acorns to eat in the nearby woods. Pilgrim fathers had done their duty to increase the population, and this meant more houses had to be built, or old ones enlarged. Thirty dwellings now housed around 180 people. Descriptions of the village as seen through the eyes of visitors to Plymouth from 1623 to 1628 give us some idea that the colony had advanced from a poor beginning to a fairly prosperous settlement, now almost self-supporting.

The Plymouth colony was much better able to accommodate the shipwrecked passengers of the *Sparrowhawk* in 1627 than it was the destitute colonists brought over by earlier vessels. This vessel, a ketch sailing to Virginia, was cast ashore on Cape Cod. Its twenty-five passengers had suffered a very rough passage, long enough for them to run out of food. To complicate matters, her master had come down with scurvy. The ship had anchored in a bay on the site of present-day Orleans, but an easterly gale had driven her ashore onto a sandbank, giving the passengers time to get ashore with a few belongings. Fortunately, a roving band of friendly Nauset Indians came by. They volunteered to take a letter to Plymouth notifying

---

TRADING TRUCK

A. Tomahawks. *B.* Small bell, very popular with the Indians. *C.* Iron and brass pots. The top one is filled with corn (maize), which the Pilgrims also used to trade for furs. *D.* Fishhook. *E.* Two small knives, typical of those given the Indians. Easily broken, they were later replaced by skinning knives to aid the Indians in removing animal hides. *F.* Arrow-headed iron shaft, used by fishermen to land codfish. *G.* Glass beads. These might be English, Dutch, or Venetian. *H.* Brass chain. *I.* Bracelet. *J.* Cheap "jewel."

Most of the items shown are typical of those found in Indian middens along the east coast of North America, or are described in accounts written by explorers and others who visited America in the seventeenth century.

THE ARRIVAL OF LIVESTOCK AT PLYMOUTH

In March 1624 three heifers and a bull arrived on the ship *Charity*. This event is well expressed by Boston artist Eda Cascieri, whose cattle seem to exhibit the same feelings as those of all new arrivals in the colony—apprehension and despair.—*Reproduced by permission of Eda Cascieri*

the Pilgrims of the plight of the shipwrecked passengers, and this was done. Bradford sent the shallop loaded with food and clothing, together with materials to patch up their ship. Landing on the west side of the cape to avoid the long voyage around its tip, the rescue party found the survivors and distributed the supplies. They had just arrived back in Plymouth when the Indians came again to report that the *Sparrowhawk* was beyond repair, and that the passengers had requested that they be allowed to winter at Plymouth. To this the Pilgrims responded in their usual kindly manner, sending the shallop to pick them up. Somehow all found a place among the families, and took up tasks to earn their keep until they could resume their voyage to Virginia. In the spring the newcomers were allotted land on which to grow crops to supply food for their future journey, which took place at the end of summer, on a ship bound for Virginia.

Nothing was heard of the *Sparrowhawk* for 200 years, buried as the vessel was under the sand. But nature has a way of uncovering such wrecks when storms lash the beach. Uncovered in 1863, the ribs of the once proud ketch protruded for all to see, exciting naval historians, who made every effort to identify the craft. They painstakingly reconstructed the remains of the *Sparrowhawk,* and the wreck was placed on exhibition, allowing visitors to see the manner of ship which bravely crossed the seas to bring new blood to America. The reconstructed vessel is now a prized exhibit in Pilgrim Hall in Plymouth, where other artifacts of the period are shown, including the very few the Pilgrims left behind. It is difficult to conceive how a vessel only forty-five feet long could carry captain, crew, and twenty-five passengers and their belongings across the stormy Atlantic on a voyage lasting nearly two months; yet it happened time and time again in the seventeenth century.

THE PILGRIMS' NEGLECT OF FISHING

The reader may wonder why the Pilgrims did not rely upon fishing to repay their debt to their backers. Most of the coastal settlements in New England engaged in fishing as an industry, which the Pilgrims never did, preferring the fur trade and dealing in cattle as their means of sustenance. Even

when the *Little James* was made available to them as a fishing vessel, they used it mostly to supply the fish needs of the colony, neglecting the European market which paid good money for choice codfish. They may have been discouraged when their one try at this market failed. Their catch, while plentiful, had contained fish other than cod, and was worth little in a selective market which valued the cod above all other fish. Cod fishing required fishing with a hand-line, which took more time than the netting of fish. It demanded skill and a knowledge of the haunts of the fish, and the colonists of Plymouth lacked the will to acquire the know-how. Furthermore, without a means of making salt in large quantity, it was not possible to transport fish across the Atlantic; and, as we know, the Pilgrims never did build a salt pan for this purpose. This seems strange, inasmuch as a saltmaker settled in the colony, but he turned miller instead of following his trade.

The crew of the *Little James* were a wild bunch, and got their ship wrecked off the coast of Maine. When repaired, the ship was sent back to England, and with it went the hopes of a fishing industry at Plymouth. Later the *Little James,* along with the *White Angel,* made a trip to the fishing grounds off Maine; the latter ship sold its catch in England, but *Little James* was pirated in the English Channel, her catch sold, and her crew made slaves. Trouble also developed at the fishing stages at Gloucester, which further discouraged the Pilgrims from engaging in the fish trade.

THE FUR TRADE AS THE MEANS OF PAYING THE PILGRIMS' DEBTS

The Pilgrims finally opted to stick to trading in furs as the means of paying off their debts. In one way this was a wise decision, beaver fur being then in great demand in England for use in the manufacture of hats. Other skins were used to make garments for use in cold weather. The Indians were the prize trappers of fur-bearing animals, and this the Pilgrims left to them; a fur not damaged by a musket shot was worth more. The curing of the hides was also left to the Indians, who dried but did not tan their skins. Packed tightly in barrels during shipping, to keep them free from mildew, they ar-

SMALL OCEAN-GOING VESSEL OF THE SIXTEENTH CENTURY

This pen drawing by Holbein (1532) shows the vessel getting under way. The ship depicted is typical of those used by early voyagers to the New World. Note the crowded conditions on deck. Ships even smaller than this arrived in Plymouth after the Pilgrims were settled.—*Photograph courtesy of Städelschen Kunstinstituts, Frankfurt-am-Main*

rived at the hatmaker's unspoiled and ready for his process of tanning, using the hair to make felt for hats.

So good was this fur trade that two of the Adventurers came to Plymouth to get firsthand knowledge of its possibilities. This being so, it seems strange that despite every effort, the Pilgrims never seemed to reduce their debt by any appreciable amount. This was because their backers charged them high prices for supplies, adding commissions that were unfair and not previously agreed upon. In consequence the Pilgrims sent various of their more trusted members to England to try to come to a better agreement with their backers. Winslow went, as did Allerton several times. The Pilgrims sent Standish in 1625 to obtain supplies, but they did not succeed in making a better deal.

By the year 1626 the Pilgrims began to think

FUR TRADING

Captain Myles Standish trades for beaver skins with his Indian friend Hobomok, while Mrs. Standish hovers in the background, wondering if the Indian will stay for dinner.

they never would get out from under the debt they owed their backers, who over the years had seen to it that all new supplies carried high interest on top of their actual cost. Even when a representative from the Plymouth colony had gone over to negotiate with the Adventurers, he always seemed to return with the news that he had been forced to borrow money for supplies at a high rate of interest. Allerton, who had been back to England several times, returned to the colony with a new agreement for the debt to be paid over a nine-year period if the backers would renounce their claim on the property at Plymouth. To accomplish this the more responsible members of the colony organized a group called the "undertakers," comprising Bradford, Brewster, Allerton, Standish, Winslow, Howland, Alden, and Prince. They assumed this responsibility in exchange for a monopoly of trade with the Indians and supplies they bought for the colony, which they would trade for corn to those in need of them. As in all such deals there are those who take advantage, as James Sherley of the Adventurers did on one side, with Allerton "wheeling and dealing" on the other. The latter did some trading on his own, selling furs to enable him to invest in fishing ventures. The Pilgrim leaders frowned on this practice, relieving Allerton of his duties as their agent. Some years later Allerton moved to New Haven to carry on his ventures. He must have outsmarted himself for, when he died, his estate was insolvent.

It was not until 1648 that the debts were paid off, and then only when the Undertakers sold their houses and some property to get out from under them. They had been cheated for years, spending much of their efforts in paying off interest on their debts, incurred every time they borrowed more money to buy supplies. Had they had among them a really good businessman, their debts might have been paid off years before they were.

TRADE WITH OTHER COLONIES

The Pilgrims traded not only with the Indians but with other colonies along the Atlantic coast of North America. The Dutch and the Puritans' Massachusetts Bay Colony, established at Salem in 1626, figured importantly in this trade. The Dutch on Manhattan Island and along the Hudson River had started a fur trade with the Indians after Hudson discovered that region for them. Allerton had made contact with them, working for their interests after he left the Plymouth colony.

Looking at a map of the east coast of America, it can be seen that Cape Cod juts out into the sea, making a long voyage necessary to reach the Dutch settlement on Long Island Sound. Since only a narrow strip of land connects the cape to the mainland, the Pilgrims established a trading post at Aptucxet (the present Bourne), at the head of Buzzards Bay. The Indians plied their canoes across this bay down to Manhattan, where they traded with the Dutch. This was a group the Pilgrims wanted to meet; so, in 1627, upon the first written communication between the two groups, the Dutch sent their secretary, Isaack de Rasieres, to Plymouth. We have quoted his description of the Pilgrim village contained in his report to his masters. Thanks to de Rasieres' praise of the Pilgrims, it was not long before trading began between the two parties, for mutual benefit.

It was at this time that wampum was introduced as a form of currency. Wampum was made from parts of the quahaug (hard-shell clam), or the shells of sea snails. It was carried on a string or in the form of a belt. The Indians used this in trade with the Dutch, who did not want the Pilgrims to invade their neck of the woods, and so sold this currency to the colonists to use when trading with the Indians in their own territory.

For five years trade between the Pilgrims and Dutch went on; then the two parties quarrelled over rights to a trading post on the Connecticut River. The Pilgrims quit in disgust and transferred their efforts to Maine, establishing a trading post on the Kennebec River, for which they obtained a patent at high cost. In addition to goods from England, they stocked this post with ship's biscuit, peas, and dried fruits, obtained from the fishing boats which frequented those waters. John Howland, who was resident agent there, did well for a number of years, but profits declined when traders dealt directly with England, cutting down on the Pilgrims' receipts. Allerton was in business at this place after he left Plymouth, but turned over his enterprise to others when he entered the fur trade. Eventually the French took over all the trading

posts in Maine, mainly by trickery, but finally in the name of their king.

Peaceful though the Pilgrims were, they did not take this lying down, but chartered a ship, the *Great Hope,* with Standish and twenty musketeers aboard. The captain proved a craven sort and, fearing to get close to shore before opening fire, he shot his cannon from a distance, wasting all his powder and shot, which caused the mission to be aborted. So, abandoning their Maine interests, the Pilgrims went back to the Dutch for another round of trading. This commerce took place along the Connecticut River, the Dutch now feeling there was safety in numbers if they allied themselves with the Pilgrims. This arrangement on a fifty-fifty basis did not last long, the Pilgrims finding it better to go it alone. Although threatened with action by their former partners, the Pilgrims set up a trading post in 1633 on a site where Windsor is now located, on land they bought from the Indians. Two years later others got the same idea, colonists from Massachusetts Bay settling nearby at the site of present-day Springfield. These newcomers were smarter traders, forcing the Pilgrims out, but the Pilgrims later sold trading concessions to others in the area. The fur trade was declining now that so many were engaged in it, but this did not happen until the Pilgrims had paid off their debt, thanks to the pelts of the humble beaver.

In the colony of Massachusetts Bay the Pilgrims saw an opportunity to open up a thriving business in cattle and farm produce, which they sold at good prices to the new settlers. Most of the cattle were raised some distance from Plymouth in Duxbury and Marshfield, where lush grass grew.

THE BARTER SYSTEM

Despite the eventual importance of trade to the economic solvency of the Plymouth colony, in its early days the colony was to a great extent economically self-sufficient. There were some tasks to which some were better fitted than others, and there was bartering for such services. This was common practice in England, where money among the poor was as scarce as it was in the Plymouth colony at first. A man equipped to cut and haul firewood might exchange his services for some shoe-cobbling, or for a stool made by a joiner. In exchange for a carpenter's services a householder might perform tasks for the carpenter which he himself had no time for. Similarly, a blacksmith might arrange to get charcoal made in return for providing iron hinges for the collier's door.

MAKING CHARCOAL

Charcoal was a fuel used by the blacksmith on his forge. To make charcoal, trimmed branches were piled into a cone, leaving a hollow core at its center. Over the wood was piled turf or earth to control combustion, which had to be watched carefully lest the pile burst into flame. This was why the charcoal-makers had to camp out in the woods until the process was completed.

EXTRACTING TARS

If tars were being extracted from conifers, there was an added task to perform. A hole was dug and lined with clay before the cone was assembled. Into this the tar flowed during the smoldering process. The clay lining prevented the tar from soaking into the ground. Tars thus produced were used to protect boats against rot, and for soaking rope used in caulking a boat's seams. As we have seen, Captain John Smith had long recommended the manufacture of these naval stores as a source of income for a New England colony.

ECONOMIC INCENTIVES AMONG THE PILGRIMS

The economy of the Plymouth colony was greatly aided by a decision which the Pilgrim leaders made in 1623. This was to have everyone work for themselves. It was a wise decision, and worked surprising results, all turning to with a will to work their own land. Some took to fishing, which had been neglected previously. Even the women, and some of the older children turned out into the fields to work. Trading for furs was left as a colony monopoly, in order to pay off the debt owed their backers.

REGULATION OF PRICES AND WAGES

Although the Pilgrim leaders used economic incentives to spur production, they did not by any means adopt a policy of laissez-faire towards industry, crafts, and trade. With everybody producing food, quotas had to be fixed to regulate the size of particular crops, and wages paid for labor were prescribed by law. As crops planted became larger, there arose the problem of converting them for home use; a mill was badly needed to grind grain. To fill this need came John Jenny, who set up a grist mill on the brook adjacent to the village. Although a mill was needed, its location infringed on the rights of others, particularly those who took alewives in the spring. Restrictions were placed on the use of the mill, and prices charged for milling were regulated by law. Jenny was obviously an ambitious man, eager to fill the needs of the colony. His next venture was a salt pan on Clark's Island in Plymouth Bay, and this product was also under price control.

As might be expected, some members of the Plymouth colony sought to circumvent the law. When caught overcharging, the guilty party was fined if the charge could be proved.

The cooper was also hedged around with rules, and the sizes of barrels were regulated by law. Each barrel made had to hold an exact amount, which varied, according to whether the contents were wet or dry.

COOPERING

Coopering was an important craft in the Pilgrim colony. Since everything brought over on the *Mayflower* in the way of food and drink came in barrels, it is not surprising that the Pilgrims took over a cooper as one of their number. This was John Alden. Like the armorer, he would have had to spend most of his time at his craft to keep up with the needs of the colony. In addition to making barrels, the cooper was in demand for pails, tubs, tankards, piggins, costrels, churns, and cheese vats. He also turned out all manner of sieves, wooden spoons, spatulas, and scoops, and such lathe-turned articles as wooden trenchers, plates, and bowls.

Every family had a number of barrels on hand, some of which were constantly dipped into by the

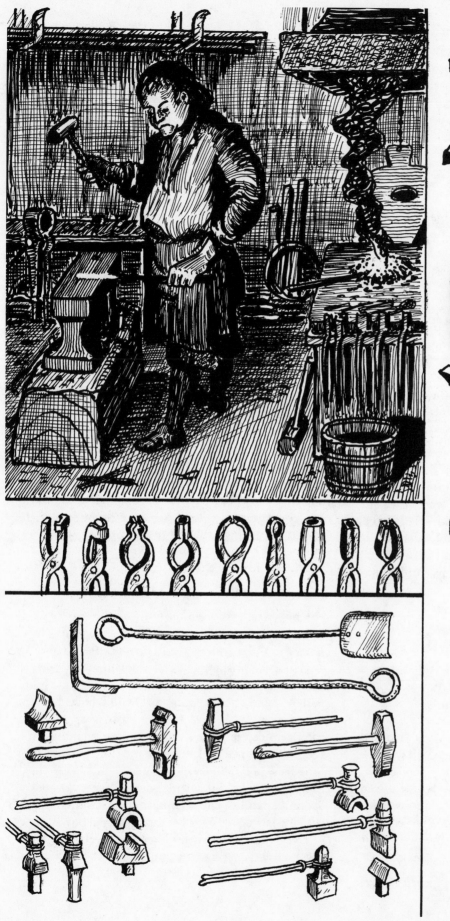

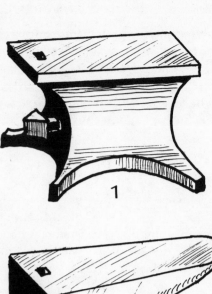

1

2

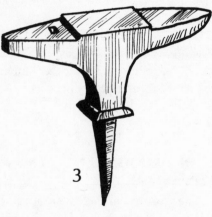

3

4

Marshall

cooks. They contained flour, cornmeal, dried peas, salt meat, and the like. This is why, in old prints, peasants are shown sitting on barrels around the fireplace. So long as the barrels had to be there, they served a dual purpose. Outside the house there were barrels to store water, soft soap, ashes, and lye. There were wash tubs, dye tubs, and a whole array of wooden pails. In the common storehouse would be barrels containing gunpowder, corn, peas, beans, beer, and furs ready for shipment on the next vessel to call at Plymouth. These barrels were quite sturdy, capable of lasting fifty years, if kept in good repair.

In early times the cooper shaped the barrel staves, and another craftsman made up the wooden hoops with which to bind them together into a barrel. Iron hoops, with the exception of those fitted on the top and bottom of a cask to take the punishment when it was dropped, were not common until late in the eighteenth century.

To make a barrel, the cooper first split his staves from a balk of clear-grained oak (no knots permissible), using a curved frow. These he shaped with his side axe, putting a bevel on both edges. He then moved to his plane, set on legs; it was not a hand tool like that of the carpenter. Here he smoothed the edges to assure a good fit when they were assembled. He gave a convex shape to the top edge, and a concave one to the underside. About twenty staves were needed for the average barrel. When the cooper had these, he began to "raise a cask" by placing the staves around the inside edge of a wooden truss-hoop. When he completed the circle the assembly became self-supporting. It was time now to set his cresset under the assembled staves. In this he lit a fire of shavings and left it for about twenty minutes, during which the wood would soften enough to allow him to bend the staves, first at one end, then the other, by using a graduated series of hoops. A barrel was now in the rough, needing top and bottom pieces. These the cooper made out of oak planks, dowelling them together at the center. He then scribed a circle of a size to fit the cask, and cut around his mark with a bow saw. Then he beveled around the edge of both top and bottom pieces, so that they would fit into a groove he would cut around the inside of the barrel at top and bottom. In the meantime a bunghole was bored at the bulge of the cask, and a bung fitted. Next, the bottom piece was fitted, followed by the top. It was then time to test the barrel for water-tightness. Should a leak be found in top or bottom (the sides seldom leaked), it meant taking out and caulking the leaky end. This was pulled apart and a piece of flag (marsh grass) inserted between the joints. This often cured the leak when the end was reassembled and put back in the barrel. All that now remained to be done was to trim any irregularities in the barrel and brand the cask with the symbol of the cooper, so that his work would be recognized. In his spare time a cooper often turned up spigots on the lathe; these were used as taps for drawing off contents of the barrel. A good cooper could turn out an average-size barrel in about two hours, once he had his materials on hand.

One item the cooper may have made was the yoke. It was carried across the shoulders, which it was shaped to fit. Hanging from each end was a chain or rope, ending in a hook. With this device a grown child could easily carry two pails of water.

The cooper worked mostly in the open, weather permitting, for his was a dirty job, his oak shavings turning black when wet, staining his hands and clothes. His bench was just a place to lay out his tools, for he worked in an open space, moving around a lot.

BLACKSMITHING

The blacksmith was an important man in any colony, fashioning things for house and home, and making and repairing tools. He was usually assisted by a helper (striker), who operated the bellows at the hearth to make the iron to be worked red-hot. He swung a sledgehammer to shape iron held on the anvil by the smith, and he did small jobs he could do alone.

A blacksmith made his own tools to fit a particular job, so that in time he accumulated a wide variety of tongs, dies, fullers, and punches, a selection of which are shown here. He kept his fire compact with a shovel and coal-rake. English blacksmiths used soft coal for their fires, and there may have been some taken aboard the *Mayflower;* but most likely the Pilgrims' blacksmith used charcoal, there being lots of wood from which to make it.

Shown at the right are early anvils, as follows: *1.* In the Mercer Museum, Doylestown, Pennsylvania. *2.* From a sixteenth-century print by Gian Barbieri. *3.* In the Smithsonian Institution, Washington, D.C. *4.* From Moxon's *Mechanick Exercises,* a seventeenth-century manual for mechanics.

Cooperage

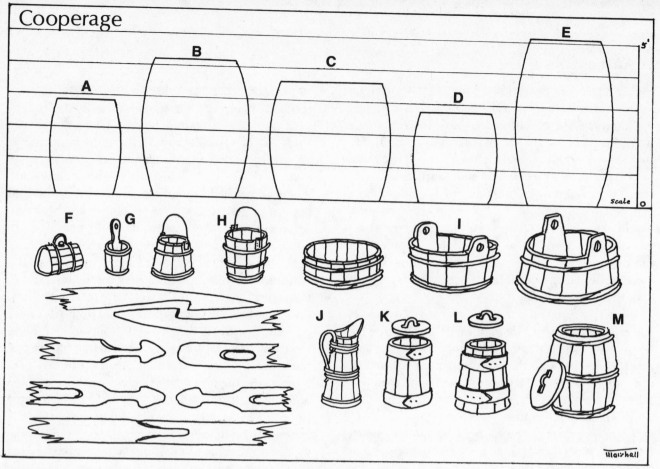

COOPERAGE

Top: Comparative sizes of standard wine barrels. *A.* Claret hogshead. *B.* Sherry butt. *C.* Double butt. *D.* Madeira pipe. *E.* Port pipe. As a measure, a barrel held 37 imperial gallons of wine; a tun, 252 gallons; a butt, 126 gallons; and a pipe, 105 gallons. A puncheon held 72 gallons of beer and a greater quantity of wine.

Bottom: Articles made by the cooper. *F.* Costrel, for taking liquids into the field. *G.* Piggin, used as a bail for liquids. *H.* Buckets with metal bails (handles). *I.* Three tubs. The one at the end was used for brewing. *J.* Jug. *K.* Grain barrel. *L.* Flour barrel. *M.* Sugar barrel.

Bottom left: Various methods of securing wooden staves around a coopered article.

Barrels made for other than liquids were called "slack" cooperage, as opposed to "tight" cooperage for barrels which held liquids. The cooper was an important man in any community until way into the twentieth century.

PRINTS ON COOPERING

Left: Setting hoops on a barrel. *Right:* Cooper planing stave. The man behind the cooper is making a hoop. In the background two men are setting hoops.—*Both prints from John Amos Comenius'* Visible World, *translated into English by Charles Hook in 1778.*

COOPERING ABOARD THE *MAYFLOWER*

John Alden and helper tighten the hoops on a cask in the hold of the *Mayflower.* The helper is twisting a "Spanish windlass" to bring the staves together, while the cooper tightens the hoops by beating them down with tool and hammer.

SHAPING A BARREL STAVE

A cooper shaping a barrel stave at Plimoth Plantation, where a coopering exhibit is set up in the John Alden house. The instrument being used is a drawknife, which has a chisellike edge. The stave is held in a shaving horse.—*Photograph by Thomas J. Croke*

THE IMMIGRATION OF SKILLED CRAFTSMEN

One problem which plagued the Pilgrims for many years was a shortage of skilled craftsmen of the right kind. Most of the Pilgrims had worked at lowly crafts in Holland, few of which turned out to be useful to them in America. The Jamestown colony had had the same problem. Captain John Smith had pleaded with the backers of the colony to send out more carpenters and craftsmen to replace the gentlemen-adventurers and urban riffraff he was then saddled with. These refused to work until threatened with no food unless they did so. The Pilgrims had some such conduct when replacement colonists came, and this at a time when none ate a full meal. Bradford was scathing in his regard for some colonists, writing: "They are too delicate and unfitte to begine new plantations and colonies that cannot endure the biting of a muskeeto . . . ."

When ships did come to Plymouth they brought a few craftsmen—carpenters, armorers, metalsmiths, and the like; all could aid the colony with their skills. However, those backing later colonies found it difficult to persuade an established craftsman to leave his home in England for a doubtful, even dangerous life in America. Thus in 1634 William Wood wrote of the need in Massachusetts for "an ingenious carpenter, a cunning joyner, a handie cooper, such a one as can make strong ware for use of the countrie."

When word of the Pilgrim colony filtered back to England via ships that had voyaged to Plymouth, there were those at home who felt that England was a good place to be from, and that opportunity awaited them in the New World. Tales of land to be had and friendly Indians tempted Englishmen who had no hopes of getting land of their own to pack up their tools and sail on the next available boat to New England. Tradesmen and craftsmen who settled in the Plymouth colony brought their skills with them, establishing mills and craft workshops wherever there was a need for them. The first sawmill, which used water power, was established at Scituate in 1640. Other types of mill followed and, for the first time, ships were built on the North River in Marshfield, thus bringing to reality the dream of John Smith.

With more craftsmen among the Pilgrims, it was now possible to upgrade their houses and add furniture they previously lacked. Broken tools could be repaired, making new replacements unnecessary or less frequent.

The Plymouth colony was now well established, and communication with England was made easier by the more frequent arrival of ships. Correspondence with friends in England and Holland was now possible, and this made the Pilgrims feel less cut off from the world they had left behind. John Smith had said that New England had first affrighted, then delighted him, and the Pilgrims were beginning now to experience some of the delights.

Chapter 10

A Political History of the Plymouth Colony

DURING the developing years of Plymouth Plantation its leaders achieved much in the way of government. From the simple statement signed aboard the *Mayflower* which declared that all should live as "a body politic," the colony went on to become a full-fledged commonwealth—a government under law. Those originally having a vote were the "freemen," the forty-one signers of the Compact, some of whom were so-called servants (bound to a master in the medieval tradition). Others among the original colonists attained freeman status if of good character. Those who came later on other ships were called "particulars." To become a freeman required a formal application. The applicant was required to go to court and swear to obey the authorities and abide by the laws of the colony. Nobody could leave the colony without permission of the authorities and his neighbors. A freeman had to belong to the Pilgrim church; no Quakers or those of other religious beliefs need apply. The

freemen did not constitute a majority in the colony, but they did have a vote which they had to use or pay a ten shilling fine. The freemen elected their governor, his deputy, and his assistants. Power was invested in the governor, and he used it on occasion, but never abused it.

The government in the Plymouth colony was simple. The governor and his assistants sat with the freemen in the General Court to formulate and administer laws, acting also as a judicial body.

PATENTS UNDER WHICH THE PILGRIMS GOVERNED

The Pilgrims were governed under a patent from the Council for New England, which received a royal charter for the entire region in 1620. A later patent of 1621 gave the Pilgrims authority for self-rule. The Pilgrims were also given a seal for use on deeds and legal documents in 1624.

THE MAYFLOWER COMPACT

IN yᵉ name of God Amen. We whoſe names are underwriten, the Loyall subjects of our dread soveraigne Lord King James, by yᵉ grace of God, of Great Britaine, Franc, & Ireland, King, defender of yᵉ faith, &c. Haveing undertaken, for yᵉ glorie of God, and advancemente of yᵉ Chriſtian faith and honour of our King & countrie, a voyage to plant yᵉ first colonie in yᵉ Northerne parts of Virginia; doe by theſe preſents solemnly & mutualy in yᵉ preſence of God, and one of another, covenant & combine our ſelves togeather into a civill body politick; for our better ordering, & preſervation & furtherance of yᵉ ends aforeſaid; and by vertue hearof to enacte, constitute, and frame ſuch just & equall Lawes, ordinances, Acts, constitutions, & offices, from time to time, as ſhall be thought most meete and convenient for yᵉ generall good of yᵉ Colonie: unto which we promiſe all due submiſſion and obedience. In witnes whereof we have hereunder subſcribed our names at Cap-Codd yᵉ .11. of November, in yᵉ year of yᵉ raigne of our soveraigne Lord King James of England, France, & Ireland yᵉ eighteenth, and of Scotland yᵉ fiftie fourth. Anᵒ: dom. 1620.

†John Carver	*Richard Warren	†John Turner	†Edmond Margeſon
*William Bradford	*John Howland	*Francis Eaton	*Peter Brown
*Edward Winſlow	*Stevhen Hopkins	*†James Chilton	†Richard Bitteridge
*William Brewſter	†Edward Tilly	†John Craxton	*George Soule
*Iſaac Allerton	*†John Tilly	*John Billington	†Richard Clark
*Miles Standiſh	*Francis Cook	†Moſes Fletcher	Richard Gardiner
*John Alden	*†Thomas Rogers	†John Goodman	†John Allerton
*Samuel Fuller	†Thomas Tinker	*†Digery Prieſt	†Thomas Engliſh
†Chriſtopher Martin	†John Rigdale	†Thomas Williams	*Edward Doten
*†William Mullins	*†Edward Fuller	Gilbert Winſlow	Edward Leiſter
*†William White			

*HAS DESCENDANTS NOW LIVING.   † DIED THE FIRST WINTER.

THE SIGNING OF THE MAYFLOWER COMPACT

The Mayflower Compact is signed in the great cabin of the *Mayflower*. One of a series of figures made by the author as exhibits aboard the *Mayflower II*.

The Pilgrims were granted a new patent in 1630, known as the Warwick Patent from its signer, the Earl of Warwick; this defined the boundaries of the Plymouth colony as extending from the Cohasset River on the north, and Narragansett Bay on the south and west, including Cape Cod and both sides of Buzzard's Bay. The Maine property on the Kennebec River was confirmed and enlarged. The right to govern the colony was conferred on William Bradford and his heirs and associates forever. This authority was not abused by Bradford, who was a wise and public-spirited leader, ready to listen to the will of the majority. He did, in fact, turn over his governing rights to the whole body of freemen, in return for which he and the so-called old-comers were granted land on Cape Cod and adjacent areas in Rhode Island.

THE FIRST BILL OF RIGHTS IN AMERICA

At the time of the Puritan migration from England, some changes were made in government. In 1636 the governor and his assistants, with representatives from Duxbury and Scituate, drafted a body of laws which were adopted by the General Court of Freemen; these constituted the first bill of rights in America. The laws covered taxation, elections, justice under the law, and trial by jury, plus matters pertaining to property rights and disposition. Under these laws the church was protected and encouraged, and towns had to provide for their own minister. This was remarkable progress after only sixteen years of colony life.

ANNEXATION OF CAPE COD

In 1630 the Council for New England annexed Cape Cod to Plymouth, paving the way for settlement of the cape. Nine years later the town of Sandwich was incorporated, and Yarmouth, Barnstable, and Eastham were also settled under Pilgrim rule. There were some problems to be worked out, however, before the new settlers were content. The Pilgrim leaders John Alden and Myles Standish had authority on the cape, the latter using an iron hand in settling disputes. The settlers were hedged in with rules of conduct, even to the length of their hair, which had to be of shoulder length. A generation gap seems to have developed even in those days, but parents were stricter then, requiring their young to seek their permission before marrying. As for the blasphemous, they were fined ten shillings if caught swearing, and the "no smoking"

THE MAYFLOWER COMPACT IN JOHN BRADFORD'S HANDWRITING

This version is found in Bradford's *History of Plymouth Plantation*. The original document, with forty-one signatures of the *Mayflower* passengers, has been lost.

edict extended two miles from the meetinghouse. Such rules were an irritation to the Cape Cod settlers, but they were not serious enough to rebel against. The towns sent two deputies to Plymouth, but that town had four, plus the governor, which gave the leaders at Plymouth power to disapprove anything they did not think fitting. Undesirable characters were told to move out of the town in which they lived, and if they delayed they found Standish on their doorstep. This treatment was administered to any who had religious notions other than those of the Pilgrims, including Quakers, who tried to move into the cape area. The latter, however, were better treated by the Pilgrims than by the Puritans of Massachusetts Bay. The more tolerant Pilgrims turned nobody away unheard. It took a royal mandate to moderate the persecution of the Quakers.

THE SETTLEMENT AT BOSTON

In 1630 there was a mass migration from England when Charles I ascended the throne, some two thousand people settling in a colony on the site of the present city of Boston. As the years went by more and more colonies were established in New England, thanks to the pioneering efforts of the Pilgrims of Plymouth.

THE PILGRIMS' INDEPENDENCE FROM THE CROWN

The Massachusetts Bay colonists had designs on Pilgrim territory, and there were disputes between the principals of both colonies, compounded by the fact that Plymouth did not consider itself under English rule, as were its neighbors at Boston. The Pilgrims, when free of debt and making it alone, were particularly proud to own land, something they could never do back home. They soon ceased to think of England as home, and worked towards establishing themselves as solid citizens of New England, even though they stayed loyal to the king, if not his church. In fact, when a royal commission came to New England in 1664, Plymouth accorded its members a better welcome than did its Boston neighbors. It was suggested that the Pilgrims apply for a royal charter, but the idea was rejected, since

it might have entailed a royal governor for the colony, whereas they preferred their present governor and status. This position they maintained until the Plymouth colony lost its charter and was merged with that of Massachusetts Bay in 1692.

THREATS TO PILGRIM RULE

Almost from the very beginning, the Plymouth colonists faced challenges to their political autonomy, religious hegemony, and military security. Most of these challenges came from residents in the colony and from nearby settlements. Ironically, however, what finally put an end to the political independence of the Pilgrim colony was its increasing prosperity. As time passed, outlying settlements both on Cape Cod and to the north of Plymouth under the Pilgrims' jurisdiction became more prosperous than the Pilgrims' original settlement at Plymouth. This spelled the end of the Plymouth colony as a separate political entity.

The Leyden Pilgrims had always been a cohesive group, even after they moved to America, but the newcomers who reached the colony in other ships were not always sympathetic to the Separatist cause, nor were they too anxious to share in the hard work of colony building. The Leyden people, plus others who had signed the Mayflower Compact, were shouldering the debt to their backers, and they resented what they called the "particulars," who were not. The latter resented the fact that the "general" (debt payers) ruled with an iron hand, denying any say in the running of the colony to those who did not do a good day's work for the common good. Some particulars who arrived on the ships *Anne* and *Little James* fomented trouble. One of these was John Oldham, who started out on his own as a fur trader in direct competition with the "general," who kept the fur trade as a monopoly for the sole purpose of paying off their debt. He knew that the only way to circumvent the colony leaders was to report to the Adventurers by letter. Oldham's reports were mostly distortions of the truth, although they did mention various discomforts in the colony, particularly the mosquitoes. What they thought the Adventurers could do about these pests he did not say, except that his own efforts to smoke them out had not been effective. He reported discontent among the colonists with regard to the lack of a minister and the administration of sacraments. This lack *was* felt by the Leyden group, which had dearly wanted their beloved pastor John Robinson to join them in Plymouth. This wish remained unfulfilled, but the Adventurers sent out as pastor the Reverend John Lyford, who arrived on the *Charity*. He was an Episcopal minister who at one time had a parish in Ireland, but he claimed to have sympathy for the Separatists, and so was welcomed in Plymouth. He was given a house and supplies for himself and family of five. Far from being a joy to the colonists, however, Lyford turned out to be a wolf in sheep's clothing, allying himself with Oldham and joining in his plot to overthrow the government at Plymouth.

Bradford, who had grown wise in the ways of men, got wind of this plot, and set spies around to ferret out the truth. The *Anne* had returned to England before the plotters had finished their report, but they planned to get it aboard the *Charity* before she made her return voyage. Bradford and his assistants boarded the ship and seized the mail addressed to the Adventurers, opened it, and were amazed at all the charges being made against the leaders of the colony. The incriminating report was withheld, and a close watch was set over the conspirators. When Oldham heard of what had been done, he became violent to such a degree that he earned the name of "Mad Jack." He defied Standish, refusing to serve under him, and pulled a knife on him when ordered to a muster. Lyford, in a defiant mood, set up a church of his own, to which he invited sympathizers. This was the final straw, and the governor summoned the freemen of the colony to prefer charges against the two troublemakers.

When charged, the two denied everything, but Bradford had wisely kept enough damaging evidence to prove their guilt. Oldham then tried to get his cronies to back him in a rebellion, but none would. Lyford, seeing the jig was up, confessed everything, at which the two culprits were sentenced to leave the colony within six months. Thinking he had nothing more to lose, Lyford again tried to get a letter off to England, but it fell into Bradford's hands. Even the preacher's wife said there was no good in the man, and revealed a rather sordid past in other places they had lived. This Winslow was able to confirm after he reached England on the *Charity,* and he convinced the Adventurers to wash their hands of the minister. The Pilgrims had revoked Lyford's sentence, but bade him leave Plymouth. He ended up as an Anglican minister at Jamestown, where he finally died.

After the sad experience with John Lyford as pastor of their church, the Pilgrims were loath to accept any other than their Leyden pastor, John Robinson; but he died in 1625. Allerton, on one of his trips to England, engaged a pastor, but he proved no better and, being deemed crazy, was sent back home. The next one, Reverend Ralph Smith, was a rather weak character who lasted six years, finally going home. It was difficult to persuade a good man to leave home for an uncertain future in a strange land. One pastor hired died before he could sail and was replaced by the Reverend John Norton, who stayed one year before moving on to Ipswich. His replacement, the Reverend John Rayner, a graduate of Cambridge University, lasted twenty years.

Oldham, who had left Plymouth in a repentant mood, turned up again without permission in the spring of 1625, and was soon up to his old tricks, which were nipped in the bud when he was jailed in the fort. When a ship appeared in the harbor he was put aboard, but not before running the gauntlet between two rows of musketeers, each man poking Oldham with the stock of his gun. Like most men of his ilk he confessed his sins during a storm at sea, admitting the wrongs he had done to the Pilgrims. Yet he truly did reform, returning to the colony from time to time when on trading missions. He finally met his end in a fight with Indians, but he was not the last of the troublemakers to come to Plymouth.

Thomas Weston, whose men had made so much trouble in the colony, turned up in person after discovering that the colony his men set up at Wessagusset had been abandoned. He had been shipwrecked in Ipswich Bay, where Indians had robbed him of everything but the shirt on his back. Borrowing clothes from settlers at Portsmouth, he found his way to Plymouth. True to form, the Pilgrims welcomed him, showing him more charity than he deserved, even staking him with supplies.

This debt he never repaid, but continued trading from a base in Virginia. He eventually returned to England, where he died.

Confrontation at Merrymount

As time went on a number of small settlements were established along the New England coast at Portsmouth, Dover, and Cape Ann, and on islands in Massachusetts Bay, but these presented no problem to the Pilgrim colony, the newcomers being friendly and at some distance from Plymouth. Nearer home, however, there was a settlement on Mount Wollaston, named for the captain who had brought over the settlers there but had gone on to Virginia. The settlers used houses erected by Weston's men at Wessagusset, which was on the bay. Among these homesteaders was Thomas Morton, a lawyer of somewhat shady repute who had fled from trouble at home; a gay dog, he had renamed Wollaston Merrymount, and not without reason, for here he was wont to cavort with Indian maids and braves after plying them with liquor. Morton was said to have given guns and ammunition to the Indians in return for furs, from the sale of which he hoped to recoup his fortune, for he considered himself to be a gentleman.

Morton's antics did not go unnoticed by the leaders at Plymouth, and they saw in him a menace if he continued to arm the Indians, who might then consider the time ripe to wipe out all newcomers to their country. They also saw Morton as an infringer on their trading rights; the Indians preferred to trade with him, since they got more than trinkets for their furs, with the added inducement of free liquor and a lot of fun dancing around the maypole which Morton had erected at Merrymount. Standish was all for putting an end to these escapades after Bradford's warning to Morton was ignored, and in this the governor saw reason. All the settlers around were asked to contribute towards a punitive expedition, and they willingly did so, a fund of twelve pounds being raised to pay volunteers, twelve of which Standish picked to accompany him.

They set sail in the shallop in June 1628, landing in the area of Merrymount on the banks of a river. Morton was not to be taken by surprise, locking himself and some cronies in one of the houses. On orders to surrender they shouted curses, thinking the modest force could do them little harm. They were plying themselves with spirits to gain "Dutch courage," but in so doing they were unable to aim their muskets properly. Morton, braver than the rest, and possibly more sober, aimed his gun at Standish, who knocked it away with his sword, seizing the culprit. All the rest, seeing their leader unarmed, surrendered, but were allowed to disperse. Taken back to Plymouth, Morton was tried, imprisoned, and sent back to England on the next boat. In England Morton wrote amusingly about the colonists, but could not rest until he returned, even dropping in at Plymouth before settling in Boston. Even there he caused trouble, and ended his days in jail.

It is worth noting that, even though the Pilgrims succeeded in getting rid of Morton, in time the Indians tired of trinkets as payment for their furs, asking instead for tools, cooking pots, and even boats. Reports of early explorers mentioned seeing Indians in boats of European origin, and on Cape Cod the Pilgrims came across an iron pot and a wooden pail, both obviously obtained from the white man.

CENTRIFUGAL FORCES IN THE PLYMOUTH COLONY

We have seen that some Pilgrims established a thriving trade in cattle and farm produce, which they raised near Duxbury and Marshfield (see chapter 9). Originally, owners of the cattle were required to live at Plymouth, and they sent relatives or servants to tend them. This proved an unsatisfactory arrangement, and the owners insisted that they must be on the spot to tend their stock. Progress demands changes, and although the Pilgrim leaders were against these moves, they were forced to accede to them. Thus was the colony at Plymouth weakened.

Living so far from Plymouth made attendance at church difficult, resulting in a separate church being established at Duxbury, where Standish, Alden, and Jonathan Brewster came to live. Even Elder Brewster and Stephen Hopkins moved there eventually, and in 1637 Duxbury was recognized by the General Court as a town separate from Plymouth. Others had already moved to Marshfield, which was even farther away. This became a town in 1636, with a church of its own and its own town meeting. In time the leaders at Plymouth began to see that ships were bypassing the village in favor of Boston, which was a better port. Also, Plymouth did not have the good farming land to be found elsewhere, and could not, therefore, support a large population. There was talk of moving the colony to Eastham on the cape, but this failed to materialize. By 1650 Plymouth was a rather forlorn settlement, although some people moved there from Boston. It could not, however, be the same with some of the leaders gone, and some who came to Plymouth soon moved away to take up land around Scituate, which had a good harbor for fishing boats.

Thomas Prince, who came to Plymouth on the *Fortune* in 1621, was elected governor in 1657, when he was living at Eastham on Cape Cod; and he elected to stay there rather than move to Plymouth. This may have spelled the end of Plymouth. The cape was prospering, and more people elected to move there, seeking land farther afield. This exodus from Plymouth was not confined to the common people; some of the leaders of the colony established farms some distance from the original site of Plymouth Plantation. These moves saddened Bradford, who had worked so hard during the difficult first years to keep his people together. In 1692 the Plymouth colony lost control of its cape territory when the former was merged with Massachusetts Bay.

We have followed the progress of the Pilgrims from England to Holland, across to the New World, and over the years of struggle to found a colony there. We have contrasted the character of the Pilgrims with that of the Jamestown colonists, and those colonists who attempted to settle before 1620 in Maine, and are forced to conclude that good leadership and determined effort on the part of most of the colonists, plus their abiding faith in their God, allowed them to succeed, no matter what the cost. This is why the Pilgrim story has persisted through the years, and became an inspiration to those who follow in their footsteps. Samuel E. Morison, a great modern historian put the story into proper perspective when he wrote: "In the great sweep of history the Pilgrims, as a people, were small in importance, yet their faith in God, honesty, and courage have lived in memory, and their influence is reflected in American Folklore and tradition." To this we can add nothing further.

Bibliography

Baker, William A. *Colonial Vessels.* Barre, Mass.: Barre Publishing Company, 1962.

The designer of the *Mayflower II* discusses ships used in colonial times.

————. *The New Mayflower: Her Design and Construction.* Barre, Mass.: Barre Publishing Company, 1958.

The author tells of his research on ships of the sixteenth century and gives in great detail, with drawings and plans, information on the *Mayflower II,* which he designed for Plimoth Plantation and which was built in England and sailed to America in 1957.

————. *Sloops and Shallops.* Barre, Mass.: Barre Publishing Company, 1966.

The author traces the development of sloops and shallops employed along the east coast of America from 1620 to 1825.

Bradford, William. *Of Plymouth Plantation.* Edited by Samuel Eliot Morison. New York: Alfred A. Knopf, 1963.

This is a readable account rendered in modern English, with many footnotes.

Byrne, John J. "Medicine at Plymouth Plantation." *New England Journal of Medicine* 259 (20 November 1955), 1012-17.

This article is available in a reprint by Plimoth Plantation.

James, Sydney V., Jr., ed. *Three Visitors to Early Plymouth.* Introduction by Samuel Eliot Morison. Plymouth, Mass.: Plimoth Plantation, 1963.

Serious students may find in this volume the thoughts and observations of three individuals who visited Plymouth Plantation in the early seventeenth century.

Laslett, Peter. *The World We Have Lost.* 2d ed. New York: Charles Scribner's Sons, 1973.

Laslett's study traces the importance of the family as a unit, before and after the Industrial Revolution in England.

McIntyre, Ruth A. *Debts Hopeful and Desperate*. Plymouth, Mass.: Plimoth Plantation, 1963.

This book explores extensively the problems faced by the Pilgrims in the repayment of their debts.

Mercer, Henry C. *Ancient Carpenters' Tools*. Doylestown, Pa.: The Bucks County Historical Society, 1960.

Copious illustrations of eighteenth-century lumberman's, joiner's, and cabinetmaker's tools make this book particularly valuable.

Morison, Samuel Eliot. *Admiral of the Ocean Sea*. Boston: Atlantic Monthly Press, 1942.

This invaluable illustrated volume deals exhaustively with all the voyages made by Columbus.

———. *The European Discovery of America: The Northern Voyages—A.D. 500-1600*. New York: Oxford University Press, 1974.

Read this book for an understanding of what was going on in Europe that forced men to look for a westward passage to the fabled Indies.

Morton, Thomas. *The New English Canaan*. Amsterdam, 1637. Reprint. Edited by Charles F. Adams. Research and Source Works Series, no. 131. New York: Bart Franklin, 1966.

When it first appeared, the book was described as "written by Thomas Morton of Cliffords Inne, gentleman, upon tenne yeares knowledge and experiment of the Country."

Mourt, George. *Mourt's Relation*. Boston: John Kimball Wiggin, 1865. Reprint. Introduction and notes by Henry M. Dexter. New York: Corinth Books, 1969.

This book was originally written during the early years of the Plymouth colony as a tract to interest Englishmen in settling New England.

Moxon, Joseph. *Mechanick Exercises*. 1700. Reprint. New York: Praeger Publishers, 1970.

Instruction in the crafts of smithing, joinery, carpentry, turning, and bricklaying is contained in this book.

Peterson, Harold L. *Arms and Armor in Colonial America, 1526-1783*. Harrisburg, Pa.: Stackpole Company, 1956.

The reader will find this general discussion valuable for an understanding of arms and armor of the period.

Powers, Edwin. *Crime and Punishment in Early Massachusetts, 1620-1692*. Boston, Beacon Press, 1966.

Containing many illustrative court cases, this book compares court procedure in the Plymouth and Massachusetts Bay colonies.

Rutman, Darrett B. *Husbandmen of Plymouth*. Boston: Beacon Press, 1967.

The author provides an interesting portrait of the early settlers and their crops, houses, and daily work patterns.

Singer, Charles, et al., eds. *A History of Technology*. Vol. 3. New York: Oxford University Press, 1957.

This volume, covering the period from the Renaissance to the Industrial Revolution, from circa 1500 to circa 1750, draws upon contemporary published material dealing with the arts and sciences.

Tannahill, Reay. *Food in History*. New York: Stein & Day, 1973.

The author traces man's search for food from prehistoric times to the present. The book deals fully with the discovery of new lands and sources of supply.

Waterer, John W. *Leather Craftsmanship*. London: G. Bell & Sons, 1968.

An eclectic gathering of facts, theories, and pictures with the purpose of showing how craftsmanship in leather developed from early times to the present.

Waters, David W. *The Art of Navigation in England in Elizabethan and Early Stuart Times*. New Haven: Yale University Press, 1958.

Consult this book for an excellent account of the development of navigation from an art to a science, with a description of seventeenth-century navigational instruments, charts, maps, and books.

Willison, George F. *Saints and Strangers*. New York: Reynal & Hitchcock, 1945.

The author traces the history of the Pilgrims from their origins in England through the absorption of the Plymouth colony by the Massachusetts Bay Colony. Serious students of the Pilgrims will find the extensive bibliography of interest.

Wolsey, S. W., and Luff, R. W. P. *Furniture in England: The Age of the Joiner*. London: Arthur Barker, 1968.

An antiques dealer and a writer for scholarly periodicals teamed together to write this book covering English furniture in the period 1550-1660. The book is profusely illustrated and includes an inventory of the household furnishings of Sir William Paget, a secretary of state in 1543.

Index

(*Note:* Page numbers in italics refer to illustrations.)